Reading Advantage 1

Second Edition

Casey Malarcher

THOMSON
HEINLE

Australia · Canada · Mexico · Singapore · Spain · United Kingdom · United States

THOMSON
HEINLE

Reading Advantage, Second Edition, Student Book 1
Casey Malarcher

Publisher, Global ELT: Christopher Wenger
Editorial Manager: Sean Bermingham
Development Editor: Derek Mackrell
Production Editor: Tan Jin Hock
ELT Directors: John Lowe (Asia), Jim Goldstone (Latin America—ELT), Francisco Lozano (Latin America—Academic and Training, ELT)

Director of Marketing, ESL/ELT: Amy Mabley
Marketing Manager: Ian Martin
Interior/Cover Design: Christopher Hanzie, TYA Inc.
Composition: Stella Tan and Ronn Lee, TYA Inc.
Cover Images: PhotoDisc, Inc.
Printer: Seng Lee Press

Printed in Singapore
1 2 3 4 5 6 7 8 9 10   07 06 05 04 03

For permission to use material from this text or product, contact us in the United States:
Tel   1-800-730-2214
Fax   1-800-730-2215
Web   www.thomsonrights.com

For more information, contact Heinle, 25 Thomson Place, Boston, Massachusetts 02210 USA, or you can visit our Internet site at http://www.heinle.com

ISBN 1-4130-0114-9

Credits

Unless otherwise stated, all photos are from PhotoDisc, Inc. Digital Imagery © copyright 2003 PhotoDisc, Inc.

Photos on pages 39, 40, and 44 are the exclusive property of Heinle. Photos on pages 9, 18, 28, 50, 58, and 75 are from Associated Press. Photo on page 49 is from Associated Press/ The Nation. Photos from other sources: page 10: © Reuters; page 32: © Burstein Collection/CORBIS; page 65: © Gianni Dagli Orti/CORBIS; page 66: © Bettmann/CORBIS.

Dictionary definitions are from Heinle's *Newbury House Dictionary of American English*, © 2002, Monroe Allen Publishers, Inc. *The Ghost and the Darkness* (Unit 1): © Paramount Pictures, 1996. SAT® (Unit 12) is a registered trademark of The College Entrance Examination Board. TOEFL® (Unit 12) is a registered trademark of Educational Testing Service (ETS). IELTS® (Unit 12) is a registered trademark of its respective owners: University of Cambridge ESOL Examinations (Cambridge ESOL), British Council, and IDP Education Australia. 2002 FIFA World Cup Korea/Japan™ (Unit 17) is a trademark of FIFA. Unit 18: D'Adamo, P.J. & Whitney, C. *Eat Right for Your Type*, Putnam, 1996.

Sources of information: www.guinnessworldrecords.com/ (Units 1, 3, 5, and 10); http://inventors.about.com/library/inventors/blgum.htm (Unit 3); http://torre.duomo.pisa.it/index_eng.html and http://www.endex.com/gf/buildings/ltpisa/ltpinfo.htm (Unit 4); http://pressroom.hallmark.com/Val_Day_fact_sheet.html (Unit 6); http://www.mori.com/polls/1998/s980205.shtml (Unit 8); http://us.imdb.com/Name?Yeoh,+Michelle (Unit 11); www.muslimheritage.com (Unit 12); http://seattlepi.nwsource.com/getaways/030499/salt04.html (Unit 13); http://catless.ncl.ac.uk/Risks/4.13.html#subj3 (Unit 14); www.polishnews.com/polonica/diduknow17.shtml (Unit 16); http://www.bloodbook.com/world-abo.html (Unit 18); http://www.tvturnoff.org (Unit 19); http://www.rodeojapan.com/e/index.htm and http://www.nonprofitpages.com/kaca/ (Unit 20)

Every effort has been made to trace all sources of illustrations/photos/information in this book, but if any have been inadvertently overlooked, the publisher will be pleased to make the necessary arrangements at the first opportunity.

Contents

To the Teacher

Welcome to *Reading Advantage Book 1*! In this book, students will find readings and exercises to help build their English vocabulary and reading skills. Each of the units in this book is divided into seven parts. These parts are meant to be studied together to help students develop reading skills as well as review new vocabulary and reinforce vocabulary presented in other units.

Before You Read
This part of each unit presents questions for students to think about before they read the passage. The questions focus on knowledge students already have on the subject of the passage, as well as questions which will be answered in the reading. Students may discuss (or write) the answers to these questions before reading.

Target Vocabulary
In this section, students are introduced to words from the reading that they may not know. Students should be able to match the words with the simple definitions provided. After studying these words, students may continue with the reading.

Reading Passage
Each reading passage in Book 1 is around 200 words in length. Students should first read this passage alone silently. At the end of each passage, the word count for the readings is shown with a space for students to record their reading time for the passage. By keeping track of their reading times, using the chart inside the back cover of this book, students will be able to see the improvement in their reading speeds over the course. Each reading is recorded on the audio cassette/CD; after students have read through silently, they can listen to the passage narrated by a native English speaker.

Reading Comprehension
This section is a series of multiple-choice questions about the passage. Students are encouraged to look back at the reading in order to check their answers to these questions.

Idioms
This section highlights three idioms from the reading passage. The meaning of these idioms and examples of how they may be used are presented.

Vocabulary Reinforcement
This section is divided into two parts. Section A has six multiple-choice sentences for vocabulary and idiom practice. Section B presents a cloze passage with missing words which students need to complete using vocabulary items from the box. Vocabulary and idioms tested in this section have been selected from the present unit as well as earlier units in the book.

What Do You Think?
Students are encouraged to think further about what they have read and communicate their own ideas and feelings about the topics presented. Answers to these questions can be used as a writing activity if desired.

There are also four review units in this book—one after every five units. Because each review unit tests vocabulary and idioms from the preceding five units, and later units recycle vocabulary from earlier ones, it is recommended that, where possible, units be completed in the order in which they are presented.

I hope both you and your students enjoy using *Reading Advantage*!

Casey Malarcher

Lions

1

Before You Read

Answer the following questions.

1. How can you tell male and female lions apart? _____

2. How much do you think a male lion weighs? _____

3. How many animals does a lion kill for food in one year? _____

Target Vocabulary

Match each word with the best meaning.

1. _____ bite

2. _____ male

3. _____ female

4. _____ collar

5. _____ popular

6. _____ zoo

a. material around the neck (e.g., on a shirt or dress)

b. to cut with the teeth

c. boy or man

d. a place where animals are kept for people to look at

e. girl or woman

f. well-liked by many people

Lions have been called the kings of the animal world. These animals can be found wild in Africa and India. Lions in Africa can go without water for up to one month, so they have no trouble during dry times.

5 Without question, lions are also one of the most **popular** animals to see in **zoos**. Almost every zoo around the world has a few lions.

It is very easy for people to tell **male** and **female** lions apart. Lions are the 10 only kind of cat that show this strong difference between males and females. A male lion has a mane, a large **collar** of hair around the lion's face. Females do not have manes.

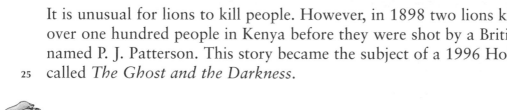

15 Male lions are also larger than females. A male lion usually weighs about 200 kilograms.[1]

Both male and female lions have very strong mouths. They can break the 20 backs of other animals with one **bite**. One lion will usually kill between ten and twenty large animals each year for food.

It is unusual for lions to kill people. However, in 1898 two lions killed and ate over one hundred people in Kenya before they were shot by a British colonel named P. J. Patterson. This story became the subject of a 1996 Hollywood movie 25 called *The Ghost and the Darkness*.

_____ **minutes** _____ **seconds** (213 words)

Did You Know?

The heaviest lion living in a zoo today weighs 366 kg! Rutledge, an African lion living in a Canadian zoo, is 1.08 meters tall.

---

[1] **1 kilogram** = 2.2 pounds

Reading Comprehension

Circle the letter of the best answer.

1. How are lions different from other cats?

    a. Lions are from Africa.

    b. Many zoos keep them.

    c. Males and females look different.

    d. Lions are one of the most popular animals at zoos.

2. Male lions . . .

    a. are larger than females.

    b. have manes.

    c. weigh more than most people.

    d. all of the above

3. Female lions . . .

    a. are larger than males.

    b. have manes.

    c. can break the back of an animal with one bite.

    d. need to drink water every day.

4. How many large animals does a lion usually kill for food in one year?

    a. less than ten

    b. between ten and twenty

    c. over one hundred

    d. about two hundred

5. Lions can live without water for . . .

    a. a few days.

    b. a week.

    c. about ten days.

    d. about four weeks.

Idioms

Find each idiom in the story.

1. **go without**—*be or live without something*
    * Robin tried to **go without** smoking for one day, but he couldn't do it.
    * How long can a person **go without** water?

2. **tell (things) apart**—*able to see the difference between two or more things or people*
    * Lucy and Emily are twin sisters. No one can **tell them apart.**
    * Male and female baby chickens are very difficult to **tell apart.**

3. **without question**—*for sure, certainly*
    * This pizza is, **without question**, the best pizza I've ever eaten.
    * **Without question,** Fred was the right person for the job.

Vocabulary Reinforcement

A. Circle the letter of the word or phrase that best completes the sentence.

1. Without question, lions are my favorite animal at the _____.
   a. world   **b.** king   **c.** zoo   **d.** collar

2. Male and female fish are hard to tell _____.
   a. from   **b.** with   **c.** apart   **d.** them

3. Her dress had a very high _____.
   a. female   **b.** collar   **c.** mane   **d.** bite

4. Be careful! That dog sometimes _____ people.
   a. bites   **b.** weighs   **c.** tells   **d.** goes without

5. Jennifer Lopez is one of the most _____ singers in the world.
   a. popular   **b.** poor   **c.** female   **d.** wild

6. I can never tell if a cat is _____ or female.
   a. mane   **b.** dry   **c.** collar   **d.** male

B. Complete the passage with items from the box. One item is extra.

bite	collar	during	female	go without	zoo

Lions are different from other cats because it is easy to tell if a lion is male or
(1)_____. The male lion has a (2)_____ of hair around its face. Lions
have strong mouths. They can break an animal's back with one (3)_____. Lions
can also (4)_____ water for a long time, so they have no trouble
(5)_____ dry times.

What Do You Think?

1. What is your favorite animal in the zoo? Why? Are there any animals you don't like? Why not?

2. What animal do you think kills the largest number of people around the world each year?

Harry Potter

Before You Read

Answer the following questions.

1. Do you know who the person in the picture is? What do you know about her?

   _____

   _____

2. Have you read any Harry Potter books, or seen the movies? What did you think of them?

   _____

   _____

3. Who is the best-selling writer in your country? Have you read any of his or her books? If yes, what did you think of them?

   _____

   _____

Target Vocabulary

Match each word with the best meaning.

1. _____ publish
2. _____ translate
3. _____ earn
4. _____ afford
5. _____ apartment
6. _____ successful

a. room for living in a building or house

b. get money by working

c. print and sell books, magazines, or newspapers

d. popular, or making a lot of money

e. to have enough money to be able to buy something

f. change from one language to another

The idea for the book *Harry Potter and the Philosopher's[1] Stone* came to Joanne Kathleen Rowling in 1990. It took her seven years to finish writing it. During those seven years she had a number of jobs, including one job as an English teacher in Portugal.

5 Rowling sent the book to four publishers before one of them bought it. She was very happy to sell her book because it was her life's dream to be a **published** writer. Before she sold her book, Rowling was living in a small **apartment** with her daughter and was very poor. She could not **afford** heat in the winter.

Harry Potter became very **successful** with children
10 and adults in England. The book also really took off in the United States. After her second and third books were published, the three Harry Potter books filled the top three places on many newspapers' lists of best-sellers.[2] Then the books
15 were made into popular movies. Without question, Rowling's life had completely changed, in just three years.

Harry Potter has now sold more than 30 million[3] books around the world and has been **translated**
20 into more than thirty-five languages. In 1997, she **earned** £70 (about US$110) a week. By the end of 2001, she had earned over £150 million ($250 million), making her one of the most successful female writers of all time.

_____ **minutes** _____ **seconds** (226 words)

---

[1] **philosopher** a person who studies serious questions about life and the world
[2] **best-seller** a book that has sold a very large number of copies
[3] **one million** 1,000,000

Reading Comprehension

Circle the letter of the best answer.

1. This reading is about . . .
   - **a.** Harry Potter's life.
   - **b.** how the book became a movie.
   - **c.** the writer's life.
   - **d.** why Harry Potter is popular.

2. Which sentence is true about the first Harry Potter book?
   - **a.** Four publishers bought it.
   - **b.** It was first published in Portugal.
   - **c.** It took the writer many years to finish it.
   - **d.** Rowling got the idea from her daughter.

3. Rowling's dream was . . .
   - **a.** to be a magician.
   - **b.** to have her books published.
   - **c.** to make a movie.
   - **d.** to be an English teacher.

4. How many languages has *Harry Potter* been translated into?
   - **a.** more than 35
   - **b.** about 90
   - **c.** about 135
   - **d.** more than 150

5. Which sentence is true about Rowling?
   - **a.** Many other writers have been much more successful than her.
   - **b.** Not many writers are as successful as she is.
   - **c.** She is more successful than all other writers.
   - **d.** She became successful because of the movie.

Idioms

Find each idiom in the story.

1. **a number of**—*several*
   - **A number of** students did not do the homework.
   - He found **a number of** empty cans behind his house.

2. **take off**—*become popular*
   - Cell phones really **took off** quickly in Asia.
   - The new potato chip didn't **take off**, so the company stopped making them.

3. **around the world**—*in many different countries*
   - People **around the world** enjoy chocolate.
   - The company sells its clothes **around the world**.

Vocabulary Reinforcement

A. Circle the letter of the word or phrase that best completes the sentence.

1. Doctors _____ a lot more money than teachers.

   a. earn   **b.** translate   **c.** publish   **d.** bite

2. We're going to move to a bigger _____ next month.

   a. zoo   **b.** apartment   **c.** collar   **d.** publisher

3. His first movie was not famous, but his second one really _____.

   a. went without   **b.** took off   **c.** told apart   **d.** turned on

4. The book was short, but it was very difficult to _____ into other languages.

   a. translate   **b.** publish   **c.** afford   **d.** earn

5. I'd love to buy a new TV, but I just can't _____ it.

   a. earn   **b.** go without   **c.** tell   **d.** afford

6. She was unhappy because the magazine did not ____ her story.

   a. afford   **b.** bite   **c.** earn   **d.** publish

B. Complete the passage with items from the box. One item is extra.

apartment	around the world	earned	popular	afford	translated

Joanne Kathleen Rowling wrote the (1)_____ Harry Potter books. People
(2)_____ like these books. Her books have been (3)_____ into many
languages. Before Harry Potter became famous, Rowling did not have money to pay for
heat in her (4)_____. But her books became big hits, and now she has
(5)_____ millions of dollars!

What Do You Think?

1. Which books have you read that are also movies? Which did you enjoy more—the books or the movies?

2. Which books have you read that were translated from other languages?

Bubble Gum

Before You Read

Answer the following questions.

1. What kinds of candy are popular in your country?

2. How often do you buy chewing gum?
   What kind(s) do you like?

3. How long ago do you think bubble gum was invented?

Target Vocabulary

Match each word with the best meaning.

1. _____ rubber   **a.** a soft material used to make erasers and tires

2. _____ taste   **b.** make better

3. _____ chew   **c.** learn, find, or find out something no one knew before

4. _____ improve   **d.** break up food with the teeth

5. _____ discover   **e.** a person who creates new things

6. _____ inventor   **f.** the flavor of food on the tongue

13

Thomas Adams, an American **inventor**, is the father of modern bubble gum. During the 1870s, Adams **discovered** by accident a new way to make
5 **chewing** gum, while he was trying to find a use for chicle. *Chicle* is a Spanish word for the sap[1] that comes from one kind of Mexican tree. Mr. Adams wanted to make **rubber** from chicle.

10 Mr. Adams worked for a long time trying to make rubber from chicle. His oldest son, Thomas Jr.,[2] also helped him now and then. But they never discovered a way to make it work.

15 One day, Thomas Adams Sr.[3] was in a store when he heard a young girl ask for some chewing gum. Adams and his son had been chewing chicle while they were working on the rubber, so he decided to give up trying to make rubber from the chicle and make gum instead.

At that time, chewing gum was made from sap from spruce trees. This chewing
20 gum had a strong **taste**. Adams thought chewing gum from chicle tasted better. He and his son wrapped[4] small pieces of chicle in colored paper and sold it. In no time, people everywhere began chewing his gum.

People could blow bubbles with chicle chewing gum, but the bubbles were very sticky. It was not until 1928 that Walter Diemer found a way to **improve** chewing
25 gum by making bubbles that were not sticky.

 _____ **minutes** _____ **seconds** (234 words)

> ### Did You Know?
> The largest bubble ever blown was 58.4 centimeters across!

---

[1] **sap** sugary water inside plants
[2] **Jr.** Junior (used for a child who has the same name as one of his/her parents)
[3] **Sr.** Senior (used for a parent who has the same name as one of his/her children)
[4] **wrap** to cover, like a gift or present

Reading Comprehension

Circle the letter of the best answer.

1. Where was Thomas Adams from?
   - **a.** Chile
   - **c.** America
   - **b.** Spain
   - **d.** Mexico

2. Who helped Mr. Adams try to make rubber?
   - **a.** a girl in a store
   - **c.** his best friend
   - **b.** Walter Diemer
   - **d.** someone in his family

3. What was Thomas Adams trying to make?
   - **a.** a new kind of rubber
   - **c.** a new kind of chicle
   - **b.** a new kind of candy
   - **d.** a new kind of taste

4. Which of these sentences is NOT true?
   - **a.** Thomas Jr. helped his father.
   - **b.** Mr. Adams was the first person to sell gum.
   - **c.** Mr. Adams thought spruce gum did not taste as good as gum from chicle.
   - **d.** Mr. Adams never found a way to make rubber from chicle.

5. How was Mr. Diemer's gum different from other gum?
   - **a.** It made bubbles.
   - **c.** It was less sticky.
   - **b.** It was sold in colored paper.
   - **d.** It was made from tree sap.

Idioms

Find each idiom in the story.

1. **by accident**—*by chance, not planned*
   - He was killed when he shot himself **by accident**.
   - Last night I found a great new web site **by accident**.

2. **now and then**—*sometimes*
   - Everybody has bad days **now and then**.
   - I enjoy going to movies **now and then**.

3. **give up**—*stop doing something*
   - Amy **gave up** searching for her dog when it got dark.
   - William **gave up** smoking several weeks ago.

Vocabulary Reinforcement

A. Circle the letter of the word or phrase that best completes the sentence.

1. Thomas Edison, who made the first electric light, was a famous _____.
   a. publisher   **b.** writer   **c.** inventor   **d.** philosopher

2. Linda does not like the _____ of fruit candy.
   a. chew   **b.** bite   **c.** sweet   **d.** taste

3. Bubble gum was invented _____.
   a. without question   **b.** by accident   **c.** now and then   **d.** around the world

4. Some kinds of meat are very difficult to _____.
   a. earn   **b.** discover   **c.** invent   **d.** chew

5. Denise never _____ looking for a nice man.
   a. gave up   **b.** told apart   **c.** translated   **d.** afforded

6. Bicycle tires are made of _____.
   a. gum   **b.** bubbles   **c.** rubber   **d.** candy

B. Complete the passage with items from the box. One item is extra.

> discovered   gave up   improved   now and then   rubber   taste

Thomas Adams was the man who (1)_____ a way to make bubble gum from chicle. At first, he was trying to make (2)_____ from chicle. He worked for many years on this, and his son helped him (3)_____. Later he got the idea to make gum from chicle. Adams (4)_____ the idea of making rubber and became rich making bubble gum. Later, another man (5)_____ Adam's idea by making bubble gum that was less sticky.

What Do You Think?

1. In Singapore, there is a rule that you cannot sell chewing gum. Why do you think this is? Do you agree with the rule?

2. Who is the most famous inventor in your country? What did he or she invent?

The Leaning Tower 4

Before You Read

Answer the following questions.

1. What do you know about this famous building?

_____

_____

2. Why do you think it leans?

_____

_____

3. Do you know any other famous buildings in Italy?

_____

_____

Target Vocabulary

Match each word with the best meaning.

1. _____ bell   **a.** go down slowly; go into the ground or underwater

2. _____ lean   **b.** a tall, thin building

3. _____ sink   **c.** not bending

4. _____ tower   **d.** a hollow metal object that makes a nice sound when hit

5. _____ mistake   **e.** not be straight; bend to one side

6. _____ straight   **f.** something wrong or incorrect

Why does the Leaning Tower of Pisa in Italy **lean**? It leans because of a **mistake**. It has leaned almost since the day the tower was built.

In 1173, the people of Pisa, Italy, wanted to build a **bell tower**. They wanted the tower to be the most beautiful bell tower in all of Italy. The city also needed a
5 bell tower because the church did not have one.

However, there was a problem. As soon as the first floor of the building was finished, the tower started to lean. Builders tried to make the building **straight** again as they
10 added more floors, but they couldn't figure out how to make it stop leaning.

It took almost 180 years to finish the tower. Since then, the tower has leaned by another millimeter every year. Today, the Leaning
15 Tower has eight floors and is 54.5 meters[1] tall. By 1990, it was leaning by about 4 meters to one side. It was also slowly **sinking** into the ground. Many people became worried that it would soon fall apart.

20 In 1998, repair works began on the tower, and by the end of 2001, it had been moved back by 45 centimeters. The tower will still lean, however, so it will need to be repaired again—in another 200 years.

_____ **minutes** _____ **seconds** (216 words)

Did You Know?

In 1989, before the Leaning Tower closed for repairs, over 700,000 people climbed to the top every year!

---

[1] **meter** 39.37 inches (3 feet, 3.37 inches); 1 meter = 100 centimeters = 1,000 millimeters

Reading Comprehension

Circle the letter of the best answer.

1. Why did the people of Pisa want to build the tower?

    a. They needed a new church.

    b. They needed a bell tower.

    c. They wanted to build the tallest tower in Italy.

    d. They wanted to build a leaning tower.

2. When did the tower begin to lean?

    a. from the first day it was built

    b. after the first floor was built

    c. after the last floor was built

    d. 180 years after it was built

3. When was the tower finished?

    a. in 1173

    b. in 1180

    c. in 1353

    d. in 1474

4. Before being repaired, the tower leaned every year by another . . .

    a. 1 millimeter.

    b. 54.5 millimeters.

    c. 45 centimeters.

    d. 4 meters.

5. Which of the following is NOT true about the tower?

    a. It was sinking into the ground.

    b. People were worried it might fall apart.

    c. It was repaired between 1990 and 1998.

    d. It will need to be repaired again in 200 years.

Idioms

Find each idiom in the story.

1. **as soon as**—*just after, when*
    * **As soon as** Ann finished her work, she went home.
    * Robert called his parents **as soon as** he heard the news.

2. **fall apart**—*break into pieces because of being old or badly made*
    * I bought this watch last week, but it has already **fallen apart**.
    * Craig's car **fell apart** after only three years.

3. **figure out**—*solve or understand*
    * Did you **figure out** the answer yourself?
    * Laura **figured out** the best way to spend her next vacation.

Vocabulary Reinforcement

A. Circle the letter of the words that best match the words in *italics*.

1. Sam *discovered* his mistake after he finished the test.

   a. corrected **b.** found **c.** wrote **d.** forgot

2. I need a new car because my old one is about to *fall apart*.

   a. have an accident **b.** be repaired **c.** be sold **d.** break

3. Alice *gave up* before she finished the test.

   a. began trying **b.** went out **c.** stopped trying **d.** turned into

4. Someone should *invent* a faster way to travel between countries.

   a. make **b.** give **c.** try **d.** fix

5. I went to bed *as soon as* I got home.

   a. then **b.** during **c.** just before **d.** just after

6. Her first book has just been *published*.

   a. written **b.** printed **c.** figured out **d.** changed into another language

B. Complete the passage with items from the box. One item is extra.

as soon as	bell	leans	mistake	straight	tower

The Leaning Tower of Pisa does not stand (1)_____. It actually (2)_____ to one side. The tower does this because of a (3)_____. Even before the whole (4)_____ was finished, it started to lean. (5)_____ workers finished the first floor of the tower, it began to lean.

What Do You Think?

1. Are there any interesting or unusual buildings in your country?
2. What is your favorite building? Why?

Talking Birds 5

Before You Read

Answer the following questions.

1. Which animals do you think are the best communicators? _____

2. If you had a talking bird, what would you teach it to say? _____

3. Do you think that talking birds understand
   what they are saying? _____

Target Vocabulary

Match each word with the best meaning.

1. _____ brain   **a.** make something look or sound like another

2. _____ cage   **b.** able to learn and understand things well

3. _____ copy   **c.** the thing in the head that is used to think

4. _____ prize   **d.** something given for winning something

5. _____ nest   **e.** a place where birds keep their eggs

6. _____ intelligent   **f.** an area with metal bars used to stop animals and birds from
                               running away

Many students of English think that learning a new language is very difficult. Now think how difficult it is to learn English when your **brain** is only the size of a bird's brain! That is what
5 some birds can do.

Many different kinds of birds can **copy** the sounds of language. African gray parrots are the birds best known for this.

Every December in London, the National
10 **Cage** and Aviary[1] Bird Show tries to find the best "talking" bird in the world. One bird named Prudle stood out among the "talking birds" by winning this **prize** every year from 1965 to 1976.

15 Prudle was taken from his **nest** in Uganda in 1958. He was sold to Iris Frost, who took
care of him at her home in Seaford, England. Before he died in 1994, aged thirty-five, Prudle knew almost 800 words in English. Prudle was also the oldest bird in the world that lived in a cage.

20 Another **intelligent** bird, a budgerigar[2] named Puck, was tested in 1993. It turned out that Puck knew even more words than Prudle. Puck knew more than 1,700 English words. In the *2003 Guinness Book of World Records*, Puck was listed as knowing more words than any other bird in the world.

 _____ **minutes** _____ **seconds** (208 words)

> ### Did You Know?
> Elephants can make over thirty different noises. Each noise has a different meaning.

---

[1] **aviary** a large cage in which birds are kept
[2] **budgerigar** a small Australian bird, also called "budgie"

Reading Comprehension

Circle the letter of the best answer.

1. A good title for this reading passage is . . .

   a. The Aviary Bird Show

   b. Interesting Pets

   c. The Difficulties of Learning English

   d. Intelligent Birds

2. What is Prudle?

   a. a bird

   b. a contest

   c. a cage

   d. a prize

3. How many years in a row did Prudle win the speaking contest for birds?

   a. 12

   b. 35

   c. 800

   d. 1965

4. Why was Puck better than Prudle?

   a. He was a budgerigar.

   b. He spoke faster.

   c. He knew more words.

   d. He was bigger.

5. Who was Iris Frost?

   a. a parrot

   b. Prudle's owner

   c. a Ugandan woman

   d. Puck's owner

Idioms

Find each idiom in the story.

1. **stand out**—*be easily seen or noticed*
   - Larry **stood out** at the party as he was the best dancer.
   - Sandy always does well on tests. She **stands out** as one of the best students.

2. **take care of**—*watch and protect*
   - Ben does not **take care of** plants very well. He always kills them by accident.
   - Sue has to stay home tomorrow night and **take care of** her baby sister.

3. **turn out**—*to be found to be*
   - The expensive painting I bought **turned out** to be a copy.
   - We thought Lucy spoke Spanish, but she **turned out** to speak English.

Vocabulary Reinforcement

A. Circle the letter of the word or phrase that best completes the sentence.

1. Billy tried to _____ the test answers from Nancy.

   a. copy   **b.** translate   **c.** invent   **d.** turn out

2. Greg found three eggs in the _____.

   a. brain   **b.** parrot   **c.** nest   **d.** prize

3. Mice have very small _____.

   a. parrots   **b.** prizes   **c.** brains   **d.** words

4. The nurse _____ sick people in the hospital.

   a. figures out   **b.** stands out   **c.** turns out   **d.** takes care of

5. The animals at the zoo live in _____.

   a. prizes   **b.** cages   **c.** nests   **d.** towers

6. I thought the party was on Wednesday, but it _____ to be on Friday.

   a. turned out   **b.** figured out   **c.** stood out   **d.** gave up

B. Complete the passage with items from the box. One item is extra.

brains	cage	copy	prize	nest	took care of

Birds like parrots have small (1)_____, but they can still talk. These birds can
(2)_____ the sounds people make. Every year in London, a group gives a
(3)_____ to the best talking bird. One bird named Prudle won this prize twelve
times! A woman in England (4)_____ Prudle, and he lived in a (5)_____
for over thirty years.

What Do You Think?

1. What other language(s) would you like to speak? Why?
2. What's the most difficult thing about learning a language?

Review

A. Find words for each definition. Two words are extra.

| prize sink afford lean female discover |
| brain copy rubber earn popular bell |

1. _____ what tires are made from
2. _____ get money by working
3. _____ the thing in your head that you think with
4. _____ what you get if you win a contest
5. _____ liked by many people
6. _____ go under the water (like the *Titanic*)
7. _____ a metal thing that makes a nice sound when you hit it
8. _____ find or find out something new
9. _____ have enough money to buy something
10. _____ the opposite of male

B. Complete the paragraph with items from the box. Two items are extra.

| without question successful now and then stands out goes without |
| figuring out inventor apartment improving take off mistakes |

My best friend's name is Jack and he's an (1)_____. He really
(2)_____ because he's so intelligent. He's always (3)_____ the best
way to do things, and (4)_____ his inventions to make them better. Although
he's not very (5)_____ now, and lives in a small (6)_____ near the
zoo, he hopes that one day one of his inventions will really (7)_____ and make
him rich. I only see him (8)_____, but, (9)_____, Jack is the most
interesting person I know.

C. Match each idiom with the best definition. One definition is extra.

1. _____ around the world
2. _____ take care of
3. _____ by accident
4. _____ tell (things) apart
5. _____ a number of
6. _____ fall apart

a. several
b. see the difference between things or people
c. become
d. look after (someone)
e. without planning
f. in many different countries
g. break

D. Use the clues below to complete the crossword.

Across

1. I think it's bad to keep birds in a _____.

6. Mike's happy because his first book was _____.

8. That book has been _____ into fourteen languages.

Down

2. Sue is trying to _____ smoking, but it's difficult.

3. the part of a shirt around the neck

4. cut or break with the teeth

5. She went to bed _____ she got home.

7. I found four eggs in the _____ in the tree.

Valentine's Day 6

Before You Read

Answer the following questions.

1. Do people celebrate Valentine's Day in your country? On what day? What do people do on that day? _____

2. Have you ever given a Valentine gift to anyone? If yes, what was the gift? _____

3. What kind of romantic gift would you most like to receive? _____

Target Vocabulary

Match each word with the best meaning.

1. _____ message
2. _____ gloves
3. _____ celebrate
4. _____ festival
5. _____ belief
6. _____ underwear

a. clothes you wear under all your other clothes
b. an idea you think is true
c. do something special for a happy day or event
d. something you wear to keep your hands warm
e. a short written or spoken note
f. a happy day or event that people celebrate

February 14 is a day for people who have fallen in love. On this day, these men and women give gifts and cards to each other to **celebrate** Valentine's Day.

At first, February 14 was the old Roman **festival**,
5 Lupercalia. Then, on February 14, 270 A.D., a man named Valentine was killed by the Romans[1] because of his Christian **beliefs**.

Before Valentine was killed, he fell in love with the daughter of his jailer[2] and would pass notes to her. His
10 final note read, "From your Valentine." Later, February 14 became known as Saint[3] Valentine's Day.

Since then, people in love around the world have given gifts and cards to each other on Saint Valentine's Day. **Gloves**, chocolates, and even **underwear** have all been popular as gifts.

15 Valentine cards did not become popular until the 1750s. The first Valentine cards were made by hand. People wrote their own words on the cards, usually a kind or funny **message**. Cards made by machines became more popular around 1850.

Now, every year around February 14, cards and chocolates fill stores around the world, for all the people who have fallen in love.

 _____ **minutes** _____ **seconds** (190 words)

Did You Know?

Valentine's Day is celebrated by three-quarters of Americans, and more than 178 million cards are sent every year on this day.

---

[1] **Romans** the people of the old Roman empire (31 B.C.–476 A.D.)
[2] **jailer** a person who guards prisoners and stops them from escaping
[3] **Saint** a person Christians believe was chosen by God, e.g., Saint Valentine (see picture)

Reading Comprehension

Circle the letter of the best answer.

1. A good title for this reading passage is . . .

    a. The History of Valentine's Day   **c.** The Most Romantic Valentine's Day Ever

    b. Why People Fall in Love   **d.** Modern Valentine's Day Customs

2. Who was Saint Valentine?

    a. a man who killed someone   **c.** a Christian

    b. a Roman god   **d.** a man who made cards

3. What was Lupercalia?

    a. a Christian festival   **c.** a type of card

    b. a Roman festival   **d.** Saint Valentine's real name

4. When did Valentine cards first become popular?

    a. about 270   **c.** about 1850

    b. about 1750   **d.** February 14th

5. Why is Saint Valentine thought to be romantic?

    a. He was killed by the Romans.   **c.** He passed love notes to the daughter of his jailer.

    b. He fell in love with his jailer.   **d.** He gave cards and chocolates to all his friends.

Idioms

Find each idiom in the story.

1. **all of a sudden**—*suddenly, very quickly*
    • **All of a sudden**, the lights went out. It was very dark.
    • **All of a sudden**, Harry knew what he had to do.

2. **fall in love**—*begin to feel love for someone*
    • The first time they met, they **fell in love** with each other.
    • It is wonderful to **fall in love**.

3. **at first**—*in the beginning*
    • Sarah didn't like Mike **at first**, but then she got to know him.
    • The students didn't understand the teacher **at first**.

Vocabulary Reinforcement

A. Circle the letter of the word or phrase that best completes the sentence.

1. Mary put on her _____ because her hands were cold.
   a. underwear   **b.** collar   **c.** chocolates   **d.** gloves

2. Irish people _____ Saint Patrick's Day on March 17.
   a. believe   **b.** celebrate   **c.** give   **d.** are known as

3. She wasn't home when I phoned, so I left her a _____.
   a. card   **b.** prize   **c.** brain   **d.** message

4. It's bad to laugh at other people's _____.
   a. nests   **b.** beliefs   **c.** jailers   **d.** machines

5. In Japan, there are a lot of _____ in summer.
   a. cards   **b.** messages   **c.** festivals   **d.** celebrates

6. _____ the lights went out, and someone screamed.
   a. Turn out   **b.** Now and then   **c.** All of a sudden   **d.** As soon as

B. Complete the passage with items from the box. One item is extra.

| fall in love   gloves   festival   messages   celebrated   beliefs |

When two people (1)_____, they may give gifts to each other on Valentine's Day.
Long ago, February 14 was called Lupercalia, a Roman (2)_____, but now it is
known as Saint Valentine's Day and is (3)_____ around the world. On this day in
the past, people often gave a gift such as (4)_____ to the person they loved, but
now people usually write (5)_____ in cards.

What Do You Think?

1. What would be your perfect St. Valentine's Day?
2. What is your favorite festival? How do you celebrate that day?

The Taj Mahal

Before You Read

Answer the following questions.

1. What do you know about the Taj Mahal?

2. How old do you think the Taj Mahal is?

3. Why do you think it was built?

Target Vocabulary

Match each word with the best meaning.

1. _____ bury   **a.** the study of things that happened in the past

2. _____ cruel   **b.** the covering on top of a building

3. _____ marble   **c.** next to

4. _____ roof   **d.** causing pain to other people

5. _____ history   **e.** a stone used in buildings

6. _____ beside   **f.** put a dead person in the ground

Shah Jahan[1] built the Taj Mahal in Agra, India, in the 1600s. He wanted to make a beautiful place where he could **bury** his wife.

Mumtaz Mahal was only one of Shah Jahan's wives, but he liked her the most. After Mumtaz Mahal died, the Shah built for her the Taj Mahal, a beautiful
5 building made of white **marble** and covered by a white round **roof**.

It took twenty-two years to complete all of the work on the Taj Mahal. Today, it is one of the most famous things to see in India. The Jumna River runs **beside** the north wall of the Taj
10 Mahal, and a smaller river runs through a beautiful garden that grows inside the building.

People who study **history** have found out that Shah Jahan was also a **cruel**
15 man. After the Taj Mahal was completed, Shah Jahan killed the man who made the Taj Mahal because he did not want him to ever build anything more beautiful than
20 the Taj Mahal. The Shah also cut off the hands of all of the artists who took part in building the Taj Mahal.

As for Shah Jahan, when he died he was also buried in the Taj Mahal,
25 next to his wife.

 _____ **minutes** _____ **seconds** (205 words)

Did You Know?

Shah Jahan (pictured above) wanted to build a second Taj Mahal made of black marble on the other side of the river, but couldn't because he was put in jail by his own son!

[1] **Shah Jahan** the ruler of the Mughal Empire in India, from 1627 to 1658

Reading Comprehension

Circle the letter of the best answer.

1. Why did Shah Jahan build the Taj Mahal?

   a. He needed a new place to live.   **c.** He wanted to bury his wife there.

   b. He liked beautiful gardens.   **d.** His wife wanted to live in a beautiful building.

2. Who was Mumtaz Mahal?

   a. one of the Shah's wives   **c.** the man who made the Taj Mahal

   b. a person who studied history   **d.** an artist who worked on the Taj Mahal

3. What can you NOT see when you visit the Taj Mahal?

   a. the Jumna River   **c.** a beautiful garden

   b. a round bell tower   **d.** the place where Mumtaz Mahal is buried

4. Why did Shah Jahan kill the man who made the Taj Mahal?

   a. The Shah didn't like the Taj Mahal.

   b. The man made a mistake.

   c. The Shah did not want him to make another building.

   d. The man did not finish the building.

5. What did Shah Jahan do that makes people think he was a cruel man?

   a. He buried his wife.   **c.** He cut off the hands of many artists.

   b. He built the Taj Mahal.   **d.** He killed one of his wives.

Idioms

Find each idiom in the story.

1. **as for**—*(used at the beginning of a sentence) to tell about*
   - **As for** the fisherman and his wife, they lived happily ever after.
   - **As for** Jim, he speaks three languages.

2. **find out**—*learn a new piece of news*
   - Kim **found out** about her brother's new job from the letter he wrote to her.
   - When you **find out** her name, please tell me.

3. **take part in**—*be involved in something a group does.*
   - Wendy **took part in** the English club in high school.
   - All of the guests at the party **took part in** the game.

Vocabulary Reinforcement

A. **Circle the letter of the word or phrase that best completes the sentence.**

1. The boy jumped off the _____, and broke his leg.
   a. bell   **b.** cage   **c.** roof   **d.** history

2. If you buy the expensive one, it won't _____ when you use it.
   a. find out   **b.** fall apart   **c.** figure out   **d.** give up

3. Some people think it is _____ to keep a bird in a cage.
   a. intelligent   **b.** popular   **c.** successful   **d.** cruel

4. The dog _____ the toy in the garden.
   a. completed   **b.** buried   **c.** surprised   **d.** found out

5. I _____ an interesting new bookstore.
   a. discovered   **b.** buried   **c.** took part in   **d.** chewed

6. _____ my new apartment, it's in a great location _____ the park.
   a. As for / beside   **b.** Beside / around   **c.** As for / around   **d.** Beside / as for

B. **Complete the passage with items from the box. One item is extra.**

find out   buried   cruel   history   take part in   roof

Shah Jahan built the Taj Mahal for his wife, Mumtaz. He (1)_____ her inside the Taj Mahal. This building is famous for its beautiful round white (2)_____. People who study (3)_____ are not surprised to (4)_____ that Shah Jahan killed the man who made the Taj Mahal. Shah Jahan was sometimes very (5)_____.

What Do You Think?

1. Do you think the Taj Mahal is the most beautiful building in the world? If not, what is?
2. What is the most beautiful building in your country?

A Winning Dream

Before You Read

Answer the following questions.

1. Is horseracing popular in your country? _____

2. Do people bet on horses in your country? _____

3. If you won a lot of money, what would you buy? _____

Target Vocabulary

Match each word with the best meaning.

1. _____ period   **a.** finish a race or contest first

2. _____ lucky   **b.** a contest to see who can go the fastest

3. _____ bet   **c.** having good luck; fortunate

4. _____ dream   **d.** length of time

5. _____ race   **e.** things you see when you are sleeping

6. _____ win   **f.** gamble; pay money to try to win more money

Can **dreams** come true? John Godley **bet** money that his dreams could come true. During his life, Mr. Godley dreamed of horse races several times. He did not know much about horses or horse racing, but in his dreams he saw the names of the horses that **won races**.

5   He remembered these dreams after he woke up, and he put what he knew to good use.

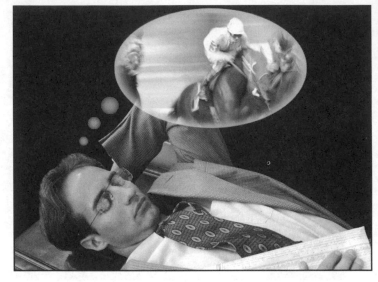

The first time Mr. Godley
10 dreamed of horses was on a Friday night. Mr. Godley dreamed that he was reading the names of the horses that won Saturday's
15 races. The next morning he found the names of the horses from his dream in the newspaper. The horses were racing that day. He bet on the horses and won.

These horse racing dreams came to Mr. Godley off and on for the next twelve
20 years of his life. During that **period**, Mr. Godley had eight dreams about horses winning races. He always bet on his dreams, and he always won.

Mr. Godley never knew why the dreams started or why they stopped. Was he **lucky** or did he have a special gift? The world may never know.

 _____ **minutes** _____ **seconds** (192 words)

Did You Know?

Three out of ten British people believe that dreams can tell you the future, and about one in ten have had a dream like that themselves!

Reading Comprehension

Circle the letter of the best answer.

1. What special gift did Mr. Godley have?

   a. He raced horses well.

   c. He knew a lot about horses.

   b. He dreamed about the future.

   d. He was very fast.

2. What did he see in his first dream about horse racing?

   a. He saw the race.

   c. He saw the names of the horses in the paper.

   b. He saw himself riding a horse.

   d. He saw himself winning the race.

3. How often did he dream about horse races?

   a. every night

   c. twelve times

   b. eight times

   d. every Friday

4. How often did his dreams come true?

   a. every time

   c. rarely

   b. sometimes

   d. never

5. What caused his dreams to stop?

   a. He bet on the wrong horse.

   c. His horse died.

   b. He stopped going to horse races.

   d. No one knows.

Idioms

Find each idiom in the story.

1. **come true**—*really happen*
   - Mary's wish to have a big birthday party **came true** on her eighteenth birthday.
   - Your dream to become rich may never **come true**.

2. **off and on**—*sometimes, occasionally*
   - It rained **off and on** all afternoon.
   - Tim has been working **off and on** since he quit college.

3. **put (something) to good use**—*use something well*
   - You should try to **put** your education **to good use**.
   - Diane **put** her free time **to good use** by working at the hospital.

Vocabulary Reinforcement

A. Circle the letter of the word or phrase that best completes the sentence.

1. My father was happy to see the money he gave me _____.

   a. come true   **b.** put to good use   **c.** fall apart   **d.** off and on

2. 1800–1850 is a very interesting ____ in history.

   a. marble   **b.** win   **c.** period   **d.** dream

3. I _____ $50 at the casino last night.

   a. bit   **b.** won   **c.** chewed   **d.** found out

4. Peggy _____ $200 on a horse last weekend, and won!

   a. sank   **b.** buried   **c.** earned   **d.** bet

5. James is a _____ man to marry a good woman like Teri.

   a. famous   **b.** cruel   **c.** funny   **d.** lucky

6. The horse easily won the _____.

   a. race   **b.** brain   **c.** gloves   **d.** marble

B. Complete the passage with items from the box. One item is extra.

bet	came true	dreams	races	won	off and on

One man had very lucky (1)_____. In his dreams, he saw horses running in (2)_____. After the man woke up, he remembered the names of the horses in his dreams. He went to real races and (3)_____ on those horses. The man's dreams always (4)_____, and he (5)_____ lots of money.

What Do You Think?

1. Do you usually remember your dreams? What do you usually dream about?

2. Have you ever had a dream that came true?

The Mobius Band

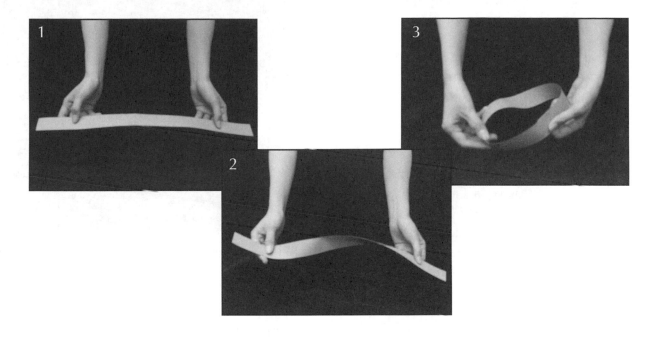

Before You Read

Answer the following questions.

1. Look at the photos.
   What do you think the person is doing?

2. Look at photo 3. What do you think is special
   about this shape?

3. Can you make anything interesting from paper?
   What can you make?

Target Vocabulary

Match each word with the best meaning.

1. _____ connect   **a.** show that something is true or real

2. _____ strange   **b.** unusual or difficult to understand

3. _____ surface   **c.** a flat, narrow strip of cloth or paper

4. _____ prove   **d.** put or join together

5. _____ twist   **e.** turn; bend around each other

6. _____ band   **f.** the outside layer of something, or the flat, top level of
                          something

Take any long piece of paper. Now glue the ends of the paper together. You have made a ring.

Take a second long piece of paper.
5 **Twist** the paper once and glue the ends together. Now you have made a Mobius band. For people who study math, this **band** is special.

This **strange** band was first made in
10 the 1800s by a German man named August Mobius.[1] Mr. Mobius studied math. He wanted to find a way to **prove** how this band works with math. Believe it or not, this band has only one **surface**. You can find this out for yourself.

15 If you draw a line along the surface of the paper before you twist and glue it, the line is only on one side of the paper. The paper has two surfaces. However, if you draw a line after you make the Mobius band, you can follow the line around all sides of the paper. In other words, the Mobius band must have only one surface.

It is also kind of fun to see what happens when you cut the band. If you cut the
20 Mobius band in half along the line you drew, you do not get two Mobius bands. Instead, after you cut the band, it turns into one large twisted ring. Then, if you cut this ring in half along the middle of the band again, you get two **connected** Mobius bands.

Try it!

 _____ **minutes** _____ **seconds** (240 words)

Did You Know?

A piece of paper cannot be folded in half more than seven times. Try it!

---

[1] **August Mobius** German mathematician who lived from 1790 to 1868

Reading Comprehension

Circle the letter of the best answer.

1. What is a Mobius band?

   a. a musical group

   b. a type of German paper

   c. an interesting twisted ring

   d. a person who studies math

2. Which sentence about August Mobius is NOT true? August Mobius . . .

   a. studied math.

   b. discovered a special type of glue.

   c. was a German.

   d. made the first Mobius band.

3. How can you prove that the Mobius band has only one side?

   a. cut it

   b. draw a line along it

   c. glue it

   d. twist it

4. What do you get if you cut a Mobius band along the line you drew?

   a. a large twisted ring

   b. two long pieces of paper

   c. two Mobius bands

   d. a short piece of paper

5. What do you get if you cut the Mobius band in half again?

   a. one large twisted ring

   b. a long piece of paper

   c. two Mobius bands

   d. a short piece of paper

Idioms

Find each idiom in the story.

1. **in other words**—*said in another, simpler way*
   - Mike is taken. **In other words**, he already has a wife.
   - The case is closed. **In other words**, the police know who took the money.

2. **kind of**—*sort of, a bit, a little*
   - Do you think it is cold today?
     Yes, **kind of**.
   - Nina is **kind of** quiet and shy.

3. **turn into**—*become*
   - The ugly baby duck **turned into** a beautiful swan.
   - James Bond's car **turned into** a plane.

Vocabulary Reinforcement

A. Circle the letter of the word or phrase that best completes the sentence.

1. I'm broke this week. _____, I can't afford to go to the cinema.
   a. In other words   **b.** Now and then   **c.** Off and on   **d.** At first

2. The small job _____ a lot of work.
   a. came true   **b.** took part in   **c.** turned into   **d.** figured out

3. The police _____ that the man was the killer.
   a. connected   **b.** proved   **c.** twisted   **d.** turned into

4. Can you _____ this computer to that printer?
   a. lean   **b.** bury   **c.** twist   **d.** connect

5. I have studied Spanish _____ for many years.
   a. in other words   **b.** at first   **c.** off and on   **d.** by accident

6. I thought it would be difficult, but it _____ to be easy.
   a. turned out   **b.** turned into   **c.** found out   **d.** came true

B. Complete the passage with items from the box. One item is extra.

band	kind of	prove	strange	surface	twist

If you (1)_____ a strip of paper and glue the ends together, you can make a Mobius band. This (2)_____ is very interesting. A Mobius band has only one (3)_____. If you draw a line along the middle of the band, you can (4)_____ this for yourself. The band also does (5)_____ things when you cut it along the line you drew.

What Do You Think?

1. Do you find math interesting? Why or why not?

2. Is it important for people to study math? What subjects should all students have to study at school?

A Long Weekend 10

Before You Read

Answer the following questions.

1. What time do people usually finish work in your country? _____

2. How often do people work on the weekend? _____

3. Do people in your country ever work during holidays? _____

Target Vocabulary

Match each word with the best meaning.

1. _____ terrible   **a.** stuck; not able to get out of something

2. _____ dangerous   **b.** large box used to carry people between floors of a building

3. _____ tired   **c.** very bad

4. _____ shout   **d.** able to hurt someone

5. _____ trapped   **e.** speak loudly

6. _____ elevator   **f.** sleepy; feeling weak

Many people have to work on the weekend. Some people do not mind. Other people think it is **terrible**.

One man thinks that working on the weekend can be **dangerous**. He is Graham Coates. Mr. Coates worked in an office in Brighton, England.

5 On Saturday, May 24, 1986, he went to the office to do some work. When he got in the **elevator** to go home, it stopped between floors. Mr. Coates could not get out of the elevator. He was **trapped**! He started to
10 **shout**, but no one heard him. Then Mr. Coates remembered that it was a holiday in England. No one was going to come to work until Tuesday!

There was nothing for Mr. Coates to do. He
15 had to wait until one of his coworkers came to work and found him. With nothing to eat or drink, Mr. Coates ended up sleeping for most of the time.

Early on Tuesday morning, the vice president
20 of the company came into work and found the elevator was not working. When the elevator was opened, Mr. Coates came out cold, weak, and **tired**. He had been in the elevator for sixty-two hours!

Now Mr. Coates says, "I only use elevators if they have telephones in them."

 _____ **minutes** _____ **seconds** (207 words)

Did You Know?

On January 25, 2000, two men fell 40 floors in the Empire State Building in New York, when the elevator they were in broke. They survived with very few injuries.

Reading Comprehension

Circle the letter of the best answer.

1. Why could Mr. Coates not get out of the elevator?

   a. It was broken.

   b. It was the weekend.

   c. It was in an office.

   d. It was a holiday.

2. What is NOT a reason why Mr. Coates spent so long in the elevator?

   a. It was a three-day weekend.

   b. He had no food or drink.

   c. The elevator was stuck between two floors.

   d. There was no telephone in the elevator.

3. How long was he in the elevator?

   a. twenty-four hours

   b. more than sixty hours

   c. from Saturday to Monday

   d. from Tuesday to Saturday

4. How was Mr. Coates able to get out of the elevator?

   a. He telephoned his coworkers.

   b. The elevator started again.

   c. The vice president discovered the elevator wasn't working.

   d. His coworkers found him when they came back to work on Monday.

5. What is the best title for this story?

   a. An Interesting Elevator

   b. Elevator Safety

   c. A Busy Weekend

   d. Trapped in an Elevator

Idioms

Find each idiom in the story.

1. end up (doing something)—*do something you didn't plan to at first*
   - I was bored last weekend, and **ended up** going to see a movie.
   - Everyone else was busy, so Rita **ended up** washing the dishes.

2. get in—*enter a car or elevator*
   - The taxi stopped, and Sam **got in**.
   - I tried to **get in** the elevator, but it was full.

3. get out of—*leave or exit a car or elevator*
   - Alan **got out of** the car first, then he opened the door for his wife.
   - Hold the door, please! I need to **get out of** the elevator on this floor.

Vocabulary Reinforcement

A. Circle the letter of the words that best match the words in *italics*.

1. Did you try the soup? It's *terrible*.

    a. very good   **b.** very bad   **c.** very cold   **d.** very hot

2. The bird's *nest* was very difficult to see up in the tree.

    a. cage   **b.** bell   **c.** brain   **d.** home

3. That dog *is dangerous*.

    a. is tired   **b.** is very weak   **c.** may bite you   **d.** wants some food

4. Everyone was out, so I wrote a *note* for them.

    a. message   **b.** festival   **c.** belief   **d.** bet

5. At the end of the long day, we felt kind of *tired*.

    a. cruel   **b.** sleepy   **c.** terrible   **d.** popular

6. You have to *twist* the top to open the bottle.

    a. close   **b.** open   **c.** turn   **d.** shout

B. Complete the passage with items from the box. One item is extra.

got in	shout	terrible	tired	ended up	trapped

A man in England had a (1)_____ experience with an elevator at his office. After he (2)_____ the elevator, it broke and he was (3)_____. The man tried to (4)_____ for help, but it was a holiday so no one was in the building. He (5)_____ staying in the elevator for more than sixty hours, without any food or water.

What Do You Think?

1. Imagine you were trapped in an elevator. What would you do?

2. Many people have a *phobia* (a strong fear) of elevators. Do you, or does anyone you know, have any phobias?

Review

A. Find words for each definition. Two words are extra.

> strange   dangerous   message   beside   cruel   trapped
> connect   surface   prove   twist   shout   underwear

1. _____ clothes you wear under all other clothes
2. _____ join together
3. _____ show that something is true
4. _____ unable to leave or escape
5. _____ speak loudly
6. _____ unusual
7. _____ a short written or spoken note
8. _____ next to
9. _____ enjoying hurting other people
10. _____ turn or bend

B. Complete the paragraph with items from the box. Two items are extra.

> end up   gloves   celebrate   lucky   found out   at first
> bury   in other words   put them to good use   take part in

Sue: Hi, Joe. How was your weekend?

Joe: It was great! (1)_____, I had planned to (2)_____ a bicycle race, but then my plans changed.

Sue: Really? What did you (3)_____ doing?

Joe: Well, some friends (4)_____ that it was my birthday, and they wanted to (5)_____.

Sue: Oh! I didn't know. Happy birthday! Did you get many gifts?

Joe: Yeah, I sure did! I got a book on history, and some warm (6)_____ for skiing.

Sue: Great. I know you go skiing a lot, I'm sure you'll (7)_____. You're (8)_____ to have such good friends.

C. Match each idiom with the best definition. One definition is extra.

1. _____ fall in love
2. _____ turn into
3. _____ all of a sudden
4. _____ come true
5. _____ off and on
6. _____ in other words

a. become
b. quickly and surprisingly
c. happen (e.g., a dream or a wish)
d. sometimes
e. leave a car or elevator
f. start to feel romantic about someone
g. to say in a different way

D. Use the clues below to complete the crossword.

Across

1. I worked hard all day and feel very _____.
4. enter a car or elevator
6. The cat climbed onto the _____ of the house.
7. a length of time
8. a long thin piece of paper or material
10. Hundreds of people had a great time at the summer _____.
11. a hard stone used in buildings

Down

1. very bad
2. I won $50 in a _____.
3. This book isn't very interesting. In fact, it's _____ boring.
5. I took the _____ down to the first floor.
9. Last night I had a really interesting _____.

Michelle Yeoh 11

Before You Read

Answer the following questions.

1. Do you like watching action movies?
   What is your favorite type of movie? _____

2. Do you know any famous action movie stars?
   What movies have they been in? _____

3. What do you know about the actress in the photo? _____

Target Vocabulary

Match each word with the best meaning.

1. _____ cop
2. _____ huge
3. _____ prepare
4. _____ role
5. _____ scene
6. _____ train

a. a part played by an actor or actress
b. a police officer
c. get ready for something
d. a place or situation in a movie
e. practice to learn something (e.g., a sport)
f. very big

Action stars like Bruce Lee, Jackie Chan, and Chow Yun Fat are well known for their skill at acting in fight **scenes**. But there are also quite a few female actors known for their skill in acting in martial arts[1] movies.

5 One of the most famous female stars in action movies is Michelle Yeoh. Yeoh was born in 1962 in Malaysia and grew up watching movies with female action stars like Angela Mao and Hsu Feng. After studying ballet,[2] Yeoh became Miss Malaysia in a beauty contest in 1983. As Miss Malaysia, she made some commercials[3] for television with Jackie Chan and was then chosen to act in several action movies.

10 Yeoh did not know martial arts at that time, but while **training** to **prepare** for her **roles**, she worked out for up to nine hours a day. Her acting and the fighting scenes in the 1985 hit *Yes, Madam!* made her a **huge** star 15 in Hong Kong.

In 1992, Yeoh starred in *Super Cop* with Jackie Chan. The film was a blockbuster,[4] and Yeoh became the highest paid female actor in Asia. Later, Yeoh starred in the 20 James Bond film *Tomorrow Never Dies* (1997) and in *Crouching Tiger, Hidden Dragon* (2000). Both films helped Yeoh become even more famous worldwide.

 _____ **minutes** _____ **seconds** (213 words)

Did You Know?

In 1997, an American magazine, *People*, chose Michelle Yeoh as one of the "Fifty Most Beautiful People in the World."

---

[1] **martial arts** fighting sports like judo, karate, tae kwon do, and kung fu
[2] **ballet** a type of dance, usually done to classical music
[3] **commercials** advertisements (on television or the radio)
[4] **blockbuster** a very popular movie that makes a lot of money

Reading Comprehension

Circle the letter of the best answer.

1. This reading is about . . .
    a. a famous female action star.   c. women doing martial arts.
    b. movies made in Hong Kong.   d. the first female action star.

2. How did Yeoh first become famous in Malaysia?
    a. She won a beauty contest.   c. She met Jackie Chan.
    b. She acted in several movies.   d. She made some TV commercials.

3. How did Yeoh know Angela Mao?
    a. Mao taught her martial arts.   c. She studied ballet with Mao.
    b. She saw Mao in movies.   d. They starred in a movie together.

4. Why did Yeoh begin studying martial arts?
    a. She did not like ballet.
    b. She wanted to become Miss Malaysia.
    c. She was training for a role in an action movie.
    d. She was introduced to Jackie Chan

5. Which of these sentences about Michelle Yeoh is NOT true?
    a. She is well known outside Asia.
    b. She has starred in a James Bond movie.
    c. She became the highest paid female action star in Asia.
    d. She starred in *Super Cop* two years after winning a beauty contest.

Idioms

Find each idiom in the story.

1. **quite a few**—*many, several*
    • The teacher found **quite a few** mistakes in the student's essay.
    • **Quite a few** people were waiting at the door before the store opened.

2. **work out**—*exercise (usually in a gym or fitness center)*
    • I **work out** every morning before I go to work.
    • She loves listening to music while she **works out** at the gym.

3. **star in**—*play an important role in a movie*
    • She'll be **starring in** an action movie next summer.
    • Do you remember the name of the actor who **starred in** *Titanic*?

Vocabulary Reinforcement

A. Circle the letter of the word or phrase that best matches the word(s) in *italics*.

1. She didn't *prepare* for class, so the teacher was angry with her.
   a. stay late   **b.** remember   **c.** get ready   **d.** be on time

2. Roger tried to *find out* who sent him the birthday card.
   a. guess   **b.** discover   **c.** thank   **d.** reply to

3. A *huge* fish jumped out of the water in front of the boat.
   a. very large   **b.** very dangerous   **c.** very fast   **d.** very beautiful

4. Did you know that Doug's brother is a *cop*?
   a. movie actor   **b.** police officer   **c.** movie director   **d.** inventor

5. I was tired after class last night, so I didn't *work out*.
   a. cook   **b.** study   **c.** go out   **d.** exercise

6. Jennifer has seen *quite a few* action movies this year.
   a. a lot of   **b.** not many   **c.** some very good   **d.** now and then

B. Complete the passage with items from the box. One item is extra.

prepare	scenes	cop	role	starred in	train

Michelle Yeoh has (1)_____ many action movies. She got her first
(2)_____ in an action movie after she won a beauty contest. She did not know
martial arts, so she had to (3)_____ very hard to (4)_____ for her
role. The audience in Hong Kong really liked the fighting (5)_____ in her first
movie with Jackie Chan.

What Do You Think?

1. What other female actors have starred in action movies? Have you seen any of their movies?
2. If you had to list the Ten Most Beautiful People in the World, who would you include?

Studying Abroad 12

Before You Read

Answer the following questions.

1. Do you know anyone who has studied abroad? _____

2. Why do you think some students go abroad to study? _____

3. Which do you think are the most popular
   countries for studying in English? _____

Target Vocabulary

Match each word with the best meaning.

1. _____ require   **a.** a printed paper with spaces to be written in

2. _____ fee   **b.** finish school or university

3. _____ form   **c.** ask for admission or acceptance

4. _____ apply   **d.** a cost

5. _____ graduate   **e.** go into; begin

6. _____ enter   **f.** need

Every year, thousands of students travel to foreign countries to study. More than 30 percent of these students go to the United States. Around 15 percent go to France, and 10 percent to both England and Germany. A little less than 10 percent go to Australia, and around
5 5 percent go to Canada.

No matter where a student chooses to study, there are some things universities around the world **require**. First, all students must
10 **graduate** from high school before they can **apply** to a university. Most universities also require some kind of test for students to **enter** the university. Universities in the United
15 States, Australia, and Canada usually require some kind of standardized exam,[1] such as the SAT[2] in the United States. Students who do not come from English-speaking countries also must take a test such as the TOEFL[3] in the United States and Canada to show they know enough English to study in English. England and Australia require students to take the IELTS.[4]

20 In most countries, students must apply to each university they hope to go to. However, students applying to universities in England can use one form to apply to several universities at the same time. Students can apply to six universities at one time through the British Council.[5] This can save students a lot of time and money. For universities in other countries, students must fill out different **forms**
25 for each university and pay a **fee** with each application.

_____ **minutes** _____ **seconds** (246 words)

Did You Know?

The oldest university in the world is Al Azhar University in Cairo, Egypt. It was founded in 971 A.D.

---

[1] **standardized exam** a test which has been given to many students to make sure it is accurate
[2] **SAT** **S**cholastic **A**ptitude **T**est—a university entrance exam in the United States
[3] **TOEFL** **T**est **O**f **E**nglish as a **F**oreign **L**anguage
[4] **IELTS** **I**nternational **E**nglish **L**anguage **T**esting **S**ystem
[5] **The British Council** The United Kingdom's international cultural and educational organization

Reading Comprehension

Circle the letter of the best answer.

1. This reading is about . . .

   a. how to do well when studying abroad.

   b. the best country for studying abroad.

   c. what is required to study abroad.

   d. why students study abroad.

2. Which country is NOT in the top five countries for studying abroad?

   a. Australia

   b. Canada

   c. England

   d. the United States

3. Which of these requirements is NOT discussed in the passage?

   a. fees

   b. graduating from high school

   c. tests

   d. visas

4. What is different about applying to universities in England?

   a. You need to take the SAT exam.

   b. The universities reply faster.

   c. The fees are more expensive.

   d. You can use one form for many schools.

5. Most universities in Australia . . .

   a. require students to take a standardized test.

   b. accept students who have not graduated from high school.

   c. have no fees for applying.

   d. require the TOEFL test.

Idioms

Find each idiom in the story.

1. **no matter (what, where, who, etc.)**—*something is true in all situations*
   • He will not change his mind **no matter** what you say.
   • **No matter** which restaurant you go to in that town, they're all expensive.

2. **fill out**—*complete (a form); fill in*
   • Please **fill out** this form and then give it back to me.
   • She **filled out** the application very quickly.

3. **save time/money**—*take less time/money*
   • If we go down Main Street, we can **save time**.
   • He likes to shop at Wally Mart because he can **save money** there.

Vocabulary Reinforcement

A. Circle the letter of the word or phrase that best completes the sentence.

1. Before you can _____ the theater, you must give the man your ticket.
   a. afford   **b.** choose   **c.** enter   **d.** require

2. She _____ from university with the highest grade in her class.
   a. applied   **b.** graduated   **c.** entered   **d.** prepared

3. He made a mistake when he was _____ the credit card application.
   a. training for   **b.** filling out   **c.** saving time   **d.** telling apart

4. We both _____ to the art school, but my friend did not get in.
   a. applied   **b.** entered   **c.** graduated   **d.** connected

5. Can you tell me which _____ I should fill out to apply for a visa?
   a. role   **b.** fee   **c.** form   **d.** band

6. I thought I would _____ by doing both jobs at the same time, but it ended up taking much longer.
   a. go without   **b.** no matter   **c.** come true   **d.** save time

B. Complete the passage with items from the box. One item is extra.

require	fee	enter	forms	graduate	no matter

Here are a few tips for students who want to study abroad. First, (1)_____ where you want to study, you have to (2)_____ from high school. Then, of course, you have to fill out the right (3)_____ and pay the (4)_____ to apply to each university. Many universities also need students to take tests before they can (5)_____ the university.

What Do You Think?

1. What are the good points, and the bad points, about studying in another country?

2. If you could study abroad, which country would you choose, and why?

Before You Read

Answer the following questions.

1. Have you ever stayed in a hotel?
   What is the most memorable place you have stayed in?   _____

2. Are there any famous hotels in your country?
   Why are they famous?   _____

3. Do you know of any famous hotels in other countries?
   What do you know about them?   _____

Target Vocabulary

Match each word with the best meaning.

1. _____ palace   **a.** tables, chairs, beds, etc.

2. _____ cave   **b.** not exist any more; vanish

3. _____ desert   **c.** a rectangular piece of something

4. _____ furniture   **d.** hot, dry land with sand and few trees

5. _____ block   **e.** hole in a mountain

6. _____ disappear   **f.** a very large house; place where a king or queen lives

There are many unique[1] hotels around the world. In Greenland, there is a hotel made out of ice, open between December and April every year. In Turkey, there is a **cave** hotel with a television, **furniture**, and a bathroom in each room. And in Bolivia, there is the Salt Palace Hotel.

5 Thousands of years ago, the area around the Salt **Palace** Hotel was a large lake. But over time, all the water **disappeared**. Today, the area has only two small lakes 10 and two salt **deserts**.

The larger of the two deserts, the Uyuni salt desert, is 12,000 square kilometers. During the day, the desert is bright white because of the salt. There are no roads across the Uyuni desert, so local[2] people must show guests the 15 way to the hotel.

In the early 1990s, a man named Juan Quesada built the hotel. He cut big **blocks** of salt from the desert and used the blocks to build it. Everything in the hotel is made out of salt: the walls, the roof, the tables, the chairs, the beds, and the hotel's bar.

20 The sun heats the walls and roof during the day. At night the desert is very cold, but the rooms stay warm. The hotel has twelve rooms. A single room costs $40 a night, and a double room costs $60.

A sign on the hotel's wall tells guests, "Please don't lick[3] the walls."

 _____ **minutes** _____ **seconds** (234 words)

Did You Know?

The world's most expensive hotel room is at the Atlantis Hotel in the Bahamas. It costs US$25,000 a night!

---

[1] **unique** special, different from others
[2] **local** from an area close by, e.g., a neighborhood or town
[3] **lick** rub one's tongue over something

Reading Comprehension

Circle the letter of the best answer.

1. What is unique about the Salt Palace Hotel?

   a. its long history

   b. the price of the rooms

   c. the guests that stay there

   d. what it is made of

2. Which sentence about the area around the Salt Palace Hotel is NOT true?

   a. It was a lake many years ago.

   b. It is white during the day.

   c. There are several roads to the hotel.

   d. It is more than 10,000 square kilometers.

3. Where did the salt used for the hotel come from?

   a. a salt factory

   b. the ground

   c. Turkey

   d. the walls of the hotel

4. Who is Juan Quesada?

   a. a hotel guest

   b. a guide

   c. the hotel's owner

   d. an expert on salt

5. What keeps the rooms warm at night?

   a. heat from the walls

   b. the desert air

   c. the sun

   d. the furniture

Idioms

Find each idiom in the story.

1. **show the way**—*lead; guide*
   - Excuse me. Could you please **show me the way** to my room?
   - When I was lost, she **showed me the way** to the library.

2. **over time**—*after a while; later*
   - **Over time**, he stopped feeling like a stranger and began to like the new town.
   - The problem will get worse **over time** if we don't do something about it.

3. **made out of**—*made from; built with*
   - The house in the forest was **made out of** pine logs.
   - This dress is very interesting. It feels like it is **made out of** paper.

Vocabulary Reinforcement

A. Circle the letter of the word or phrase that best matches the word(s) in *italics*.

1. The bear found a *cave* in the side of the mountain and slept there during the winter.
   a. cage   **b.** hole   **c.** desert   **d.** surface

2. I know where this office is. Let me *show you the way*.
   a. connect you   **b.** guide you   **c.** shout at you   **d.** disappear from you

3. The *palace* is only open for tours between 10 A.M. and 5 P.M.
   a. bell tower   **b.** bird's nest   **c.** gum's taste   **d.** king's home

4. I want to put a *marble* fireplace in the living room.
   a. stone   **b.** strong   **c.** male   **d.** unique

5. I also need to get some new *chairs and tables* for the living room.
   a. blocks   **b.** stones   **c.** furniture   **d.** marble

6. This plant is found only in *deserts*.
   a. forests   **b.** caves   **c.** dry areas   **d.** zoos

B. Complete the passage with items from the box. One item is extra.

blocks	desert	disappear	made out of	palace	unique

There is a (1)_____ hotel in Bolivia made of salt. The hotel is in the middle of a salt (2)_____. One man had the idea to make a hotel there. The hotel is unique because the walls are (3)_____ salt. The man cut big (4)_____ of salt from the floor of the desert. He used the blocks to make the walls, roof, tables, beds, and bar for the Salt (5)_____ Hotel.

What Do You Think?

1. Would you like to stay in the Salt Palace Hotel? Why or why not?
2. If you could design your own hotel, what would it be like? What would be special about it?

Trying Again

Before You Read

Answer the following questions.

1. What do you think is the best way to meet a future husband or wife?

    _____

2. Do you think that you will get married one day? At what age?

    _____

3. Do many married couples in your country end up divorcing each other?

    _____

Target Vocabulary

Match each word with the best meaning.

1. _____ couple   **a.** a set of instructions for computer

2. _____ (to) date   **b.** legal joining of a man and woman

3. _____ divorce   **c.** two people who are dating or are married

4. _____ marriage   **d.** go out together for romance

5. _____ match   **e.** people or things that go well together

6. _____ program   **f.** legal ending of a marriage

Marriage does not always work out. Or at least, some people *think* their marriage is not working out. One of these people was a Turkish man, Suleyman Guresci.

Mr. Guresci and his wife were married for twenty-one years, but he thought that his marriage was not working. He wanted to break up with his wife, Nesrin
5   Caglasas. After six years in court,[1] the **couple** finally got a **divorce**.

After the divorce, Mr. Guresci wanted to quickly find a new wife, so he went to a computer **dating** agency to help him look for one. He told the dating agency the kind of
10   woman he wanted to marry, and the computer began looking for a good **match** for him.

After looking at 2,000 women, the computer found only one who matched well with the man. The computer's **program** showed that Mr.
15   Guresci and this woman were made for each other. The woman was Nesrin Caglasas—Mr. Guresci's ex-wife.

When he heard who the computer had matched him with, Mr. Guresci asked his ex-wife to remarry him. Before their second marriage, Mr. Guresci told his friends
20   that he would be more understanding this time.

_____ **minutes** _____ **seconds** (193 words)

Did You Know?

Until he died in 1997, Glynn "Scotty" Wolfe was the most married man in the world. He was married 28 times—and divorced 27 times. His shortest marriage lasted only 36 hours!

---

[1] **court** a place where legal decisions are made

Reading Comprehension

Circle the letter of the best answer.

1. This reading passage is about . . .

    a. how to get a divorce.

    b. how to live together.

    c. marriage in Turkey.

    d. one couple's marriage.

2. Why did Mr. Guresci want a divorce?

    a. His wife wanted one.

    b. He thought his marriage wasn't working.

    c. A computer found a new wife for him.

    d. His wife went to a computer dating agency.

3. How long did it take Mr. and Mrs. Guresci to get a divorce?

    a. two years

    b. six years

    c. twenty-one years

    d. The passage doesn't say.

4. Who told Mr. Guresci that Nesrin Caglasas was his perfect match?

    a. a computer

    b. his friends

    c. his ex-wife

    d. his family

5. What sentence about Nesrin Caglasas is NOT true?

    a. She was Mr. Guresci's ex-wife.

    b. She was a computer programmer.

    c. She agreed to marry her ex-husband.

    d. She used a computer dating agency.

Idioms

Find each idiom in the story.

1. **work out**—*finish or solve in a good way*
    • Did you **work out** the problem with your parents?
    • Bill and Hillary's marriage didn't **work out**, and they got divorced.

2. **(be) made for each other**—*be a good match for dating or marriage*
    • I think that Bill and I **are made for each other**.
    • Nancy always says that her mother and father **were made for each other**.

3. **break up (with someone)**—*separate from a boyfriend or girlfriend*
    • I just heard that Laura **broke up with** George.
    • Things weren't working out with Jack, so we **broke up**.

Vocabulary Reinforcement

A. Circle the letter of the word or phrase that best completes the sentence.

1. Do you think this shirt _____ these pants?

  a. disappears   **b.** matches   **c.** is made out of   **d.** dates

2. Sam and Michelle make a great couple. They're really _____.

  a. match   **b.** fall in love   **c.** put to good use   **d.** made for each other

3. I was sad to hear that Rob and Sue _____.

  a. worked out   **b.** filled out   **c.** fell in love   **d.** broke up

4. Can you show me how to use this _____?

  a. message   **b.** surface   **c.** program   **d.** fee

5. Her parents have a great _____.

  a. marriage   **b.** match   **c.** divorce   **d.** date

6. My sister is _____ a really intelligent guy at the moment.

  a. dating   **b.** matching   **c.** expanding   **d.** working out

B. Complete the passage with items from the box. One item is extra.

couple	dating	divorce	match	break up	working out

A man in Turkey thought his marriage was not (1)_____. He wanted to

(2)_____ his wife. After his divorce, the man went to a computer

(3)_____ service to find another wife. The computer program found his perfect

(4)_____—his ex-wife! The (5)_____ decided to get married again.

What Do You Think?

1. What are good reasons for breaking up with, or divorcing, someone?

2. Describe your ideal partner. What qualities would he or she have?

The Mona Lisa 15

Before You Read

Answer the following questions.

1. What do you know about this painting?

   _____

   _____

2. Why do you think it is so famous?

   _____

   _____

3. Do you know any other famous paintings? What do you know about them?

   _____

   _____

Target Vocabulary

Match each word with the best meaning.

1. _____ portrait
2. _____ museum
3. _____ visitor
4. _____ hide
5. _____ steal
6. _____ valuable

a. to take something from someone without asking

b. a painting of a person

c. put something where people can't find it

d. a place that shows valuable art or historical objects

e. worth a lot of money

f. a tourist

Leonardo da Vinci[1] began painting the Mona Lisa, one of the most famous paintings of all time, in 1503. He was working on a special painting for a church at the time, but it was not
5 going well. The woman who can be seen in the Mona Lisa is said to be Madonna Lisa del Giocondo. She was the wife of an Italian businessman who asked da Vinci to paint a **portrait** of her.

10 After da Vinci finished the painting in 1506 he was invited by the French King, Francois I, to visit France, and he took the painting with him. Today the Mona Lisa is kept in the Louvre, an art **museum** in Paris, and it is seen by about six
15 million **visitors** a year.

The painting measures only 77 centimeters by 53 centimeters and is painted with oil on wood. In 1911, it was **stolen** by a worker at the Louvre, Vincenzo Peruggia, who took it out of the museum by **hiding** it under his coat. Two years later police found the painting under Peruggia's bed after he tried to sell it.

20 In 1962, the Mona Lisa was taken to Washington and New York for an exhibition.[2] For the journey, it was insured[3] for 100 million dollars, making it the most **valuable** painting ever!

_____ **minutes** _____ **seconds** (217 words)

Did You Know?

Leonardo da Vinci (pictured above) is said to have been very strong. People say he was able to twist a horseshoe with one hand!

---

[1] **Leonardo da Vinci (1452–1519)** a famous Italian architect, inventor, engineer, sculptor, and painter
[2] **exhibition** a display (e.g., of art)
[3] **insure** arrange to get money if something is broken or stolen

Reading Comprehension

Circle the letter of the best answer.

1. What is the best title for this passage?

    a. Leonardo da Vinci—an Interesting Painter

    b. The Louvre—a Famous French Art Museum

    c. Vincenzo Peruggia—the Man Who Stole the Mona Lisa

    d. The Mona Lisa—the Most Valuable Painting of All Time

2. When did Leonardo da Vinci finish painting the Mona Lisa?

    a. 1503   **c.** 1911

    b. 1506   **d.** 1962

3. Who is Madonna Lisa del Giocondo said to be?

    a. the painter of the Mona Lisa

    b. the woman in the painting

    c. the wife of the French king

    d. the woman who asked da Vinci to paint the Mona Lisa.

4. Why did da Vinci go to France?

    a. to visit the Louvre   **c.** He was invited by Francois I.

    b. to paint the Mona Lisa   **d.** He was invited by Madonna Lisa del Giocondo.

5. What sentence about Vincenzo Peruggia is NOT true?

    a. He worked in an art museum.   **c.** He sold the painting.

    b. He stole the Mona Lisa.   **d.** He hid the painting under his bed.

Idioms

Find each idiom in the story.

1. **said to (be)**—*thought by many people to (be)*
    * Prudle the parrot was **said to** know over 800 English words.
    * Rick's dad is **said to** earn 2 million dollars a year.

2. **go well**—*succeed*
    * Rebecca's new job is **going** really **well**. She's very happy.
    * The course I'm studying isn't **going** very **well**. It's too difficult.

3. **of all time**—*ever; in history*
    * Many people think Pele is the best soccer player **of all time**.
    * The tallest man **of all time** was 2.72 meters tall.

Vocabulary Reinforcement

A. **Circle the letter of the word or phrase that best completes the sentence.**

1. Be careful with this glass. It's really _____.

   a. intelligent   **b.** fee   **c.** valuable   **d.** insured

2. That's a great _____ of Kimberley. It looks just like her.

   a. program   **b.** desert   **c.** exhibition   **d.** portrait

3. The race _____ for Rupert. He won!

   a. went well   **b.** expanded   **c.** matched   **d.** stole

4. New York is famous for its _____.

   a. visitors   **b.** museums   **c.** caves   **d.** palaces

5. My new bicycle was _____ from in front of my house.

   a. hidden   **b.** disappeared   **c.** stolen   **d.** invited

6. My grandmother didn't like banks so she _____ money in her home.

   a. hid   **b.** stole   **c.** worked out   **d.** put to good use

B. **Complete the passage with items from the box. One item is extra.**

hidden   stolen   valuable   said to be   visitors   of all time

The Mona Lisa, a portrait (1)_____ of a woman called Madonna Lisa del Giocondo, is the most famous painting (2)_____. Six million (3)_____ see it every year. It was (4)_____ in 1911, but the police found it (5)_____ under a museum worker's bed.

What Do You Think?

1. What is the most famous work of art in your country?

2. What do you think are the three best works of art in the world?

Review

A. Find words for each definition. Two words are extra.

portrait	block	furniture	program	match	visitor
valuable	disappear	hide	divorce	surface	bury

1. _____ put a dead person in the ground
2. _____ chairs, tables, beds, and so on
3. _____ tourist; someone who comes to your house
4. _____ put something where people can't find it
5. _____ legally end a marriage
6. _____ expensive or important
7. _____ a painting of a person
8. _____ go away, go from sight
9. _____ instructions for a computer
10. _____ the outside layer of something, or the top level of something

B. Complete the paragraph with items from the box. Two items are extra.

couple	disappeared	over time	graduated	showing the way
dating	divorce	made for each other	working out	get married

As soon as Bill and Sally met each other in college they knew they were (1)_____.
They started (2)_____, and then, after they (3)_____ from university, the
(4)_____ decided to (5)_____. Sadly, (6)_____, they started to
see that their marriage wasn't (7)_____. They decided to get a (8)_____.

C. Match each idiom with the best definition. One definition is extra.

1. _____ of all time
2. _____ work out
3. _____ quite a few
4. _____ break up with
5. _____ go well
6. _____ show the way

a. many
b. give someone directions
c. exercise at a gym or sports center
d. ever; in history
e. stop dating a boyfriend or girlfriend
f. built from
g. succeed; do well

D. Use the clues below to complete the crossword.

Across

2. Last night, thieves _____ a lot of money from the bank.
3. join (a university)
4. police officer
8. need
9. a king or queen's home
11. Please fill out this _____ and return it to me when you're finished.
12. place where you can see art or valuable old things

Down

1. You have to pay a large _____ to enter that university.
2. I really enjoyed the last fight _____ in that action movie.
5. get ready
6. very big
7. If you want to go to that university, you need to _____ soon.
8. an actor's part in a film
10. a hole in a mountain

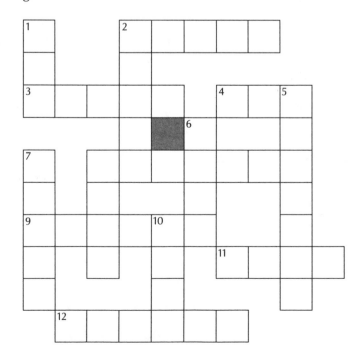

Breakfast in America

Before You Read

Answer the following questions.

1. What breakfast foods are popular in your country? _____

2. What do you usually eat for breakfast? _____

3. What do you think Americans eat for breakfast? _____

Target Vocabulary

Match each word with the best meaning.

1. _____ actually   **a.** very old

2. _____ war   **b.** in fact; really

3. _____ serve   **c.** give food (e.g., in a restaurant)

4. _____ traditional   **d.** a fight between different groups or countries

5. _____ ancient   **e.** instructions for preparing food

6. _____ recipe   **f.** passed from old people in a culture to young people

Popular breakfast foods in the United States, as in many other countries around the world, include coffee, milk, juice, eggs, and bread. Some other breakfast items **served** in the United States
5 are thought by many to be **traditionally** American. However, they **actually** come from other cultures.

A very popular breakfast food in America is the pancake—a thin, flat cake made out of flour and
10 often served with maple syrup.[1] The idea of the pancake is very old. In fact, pancakes were made long ago in **ancient** China.

Bagels, a round thick bread with a hole in the middle, are also popular for breakfast in America. Polish people in the late 1600s came up with the idea for
15 the first bagels and this new kind of bread soon took off across Eastern Europe.

In the late 1800s, thousands of Jews[2] from Eastern Europe traveled to the United States and brought the **recipe** for bagels with them. Today, New York bagels are said to be the best in the world. Many people have them with cream cheese for breakfast on the go.

20 Doughnuts (usually spelled "donut" in the United States) came from France. They were served to American soldiers in France during World War I.[3] After the **war**, American soldiers asked cooks in the United States to make doughnuts for them. Now, served with coffee, they are a very popular breakfast food across the United States.

_____ **minutes** _____ **seconds** (240 words)

> ## Did You Know?
>
> In Poland, hot beer soup, known as *Zupa z Piwa na Goraco*, used to be the most common breakfast. It was served with blocks of cheese.

[1] **maple syrup** a sweet liquid from the maple tree; maple syrup is very common in Canada
[2] **Jews** people who belong to the Jewish religion
[3] **World War I (1914–1918)** a major war between the Allies (the United States, Britain, Australia, etc.) and the Austro-Hungarian Empire, Germany, etc.

Reading Comprehension

Circle the letter of the best answer.

1. This reading is mainly about . . .

   a. famous places to eat breakfast.

   b. why people in the United States eat breakfast.

   c. the most popular types of pancakes in the United States.

   d. the history of popular breakfast foods in the United States.

2. The oldest breakfast food in the passage is . . .

   a. the pancake.

   b. the bagel.

   c. the doughnut.

   d. The passage doesn't say.

3. Which sentence is true for both bagels and donuts?

   a. They both came from Europe.

   b. They are both sweet.

   c. They are both easy to make.

   d. People in New York make them best.

4. Who brought bagels to America?

   a. Polish people

   b. Chinese people

   c. Jewish people

   d. American soldiers

5. Who served donuts to American soldiers during World War I?

   a. French people

   b. other American soldiers

   c. Jewish people

   d. cooks from the United States

Idioms

Find each idiom in the story.

1. **on the go**—*busy; in a hurry; moving*
   - I'm really tired. I've been **on the go** all day.
   - She's always **on the go**. She needs to learn to relax.

2. **long ago**—*in the past; a long time ago*
   - **Long ago**, Ireland was completely covered by forest.
   - People came to this country in ships **long ago**.

3. **come up with**—*invent*
   - I'm trying to **come up with** a name for my new dog.
   - Thomas Edison **came up with** a lot of great inventions.

Vocabulary Reinforcement

A. Circle the letter of the word or phrase that best completes the sentence.

1. People think Arthur is very serious, but _____ he's quite funny.
   a. in other words   **b.** actually   **c.** as for   **d.** no matter

2. This restaurant doesn't _____ wine or beer.
   a. serve   **b.** cook   **c.** recipe   **d.** hide

3. *Kabuki* is a kind of _____ Japanese theater.
   a. long ago   **b.** celebrate   **c.** festival   **d.** traditional

4. This apple pie is from an old family _____.
   a. serve   **b.** recipe   **c.** ancient   **d.** portrait

5. I wish I could _____ a good reason to stay home today.
   a. look for   **b.** show the way   **c.** come up with   **d.** be into

6. Tony's grandfather was killed in the _____.
   a. by accident   **b.** long ago   **c.** portrait   **d.** war

B. Complete the passage with items from the box. One item is extra.

came up with   on the go   long ago   recipe   actually   ancient

Pancakes, bagels, and donuts are three American breakfast foods that (1)_____
come from other cultures. Pancakes are a very old food. They were eaten
(2)_____ in (3)_____ China. Polish people (4)_____ the idea
for bagels in the 1600s. They are a very popular food for people eating (5)_____.

What Do You Think?

1. Do you know the origin of any breakfast dishes in your country?
2. If you had a restaurant, what kinds of food would you serve?

The World Cup 17

Before You Read

Answer the following questions.

1. Did you watch any matches in the last World Cup tournament?

2. Was the team from your country in the tournament? How successful were they?

3. Do you remember which teams did well in the tournament?

Target Vocabulary

Match each word with the best meaning.

1. _____ beat   **a.** game

2. _____ final   **b.** set of games to find the best player or team

3. _____ match   **c.** last

4. _____ record   **d.** do better than; win against (someone or something)

5. _____ score   **e.** best in history

6. _____ tournament   **f.** make a point or goal

Reading Passage 🔊 Track 17

Every four years, the world turns its attention to the soccer[1] World Cup. The most successful teams in the **tournament** have traditionally come from South America and Europe. However, over the years, there have been a number of
5 surprising results.

In a famous **match** in 1950, the USA came up against England, one of the favorites to win the tournament. Many of the American players were amateurs[2] from
10 college teams. Surprisingly, the USA won 1–0. Other World Cup surprises were North Korea's win over Italy in 1966, and Cameroon's win over Argentina in 1990.

The 2002 FIFA[3] World Cup stands out as
15 probably the most surprising World Cup of all time. In the opening match, Senegal surprised everyone by **beating** France, the World Cup winner in 1998. Japan then beat Russia, the USA beat Portugal, and South Korea beat Italy, Spain, Poland, and Portugal. South Korea made it all the
20 way to the **final** four, before finally losing to Germany.

In the final game, which was watched by 1 billion[4] people around the world, Brazil ended up winning 2–0 against Germany. Brazil set a World Cup **record** by becoming the first team to win seven games in a row. And Brazil's most talented player, Ronaldo, **scored** eight goals in one tournament—more than any other
25 player since 1970.

✊ _____ **minutes** _____ **seconds** (217 words)

Did You Know?

In 1966, the World Cup prize was stolen in London. A few days later it was discovered under a bush in a garden by a dog named "Pickles."

---

[1] **soccer** also known as "football" in many parts of the world
[2] **amateurs** people who do activities, such as sports, for fun and without pay
[3] **FIFA** the world soccer organization (Fédération Internationale de Football Association)
[4] **billion** one thousand million (1,000,000,000)

Reading Comprehension

Circle the letter of the best answer.

1. What is the best title for this passage?

   a. How the World Cup Is Played

   b. The History of Soccer

   c. The Greatest World Cup Players of All Time

   d. Surprises in the World Cup

2. According to the reading, which team has NOT had a surprising win in a World Cup match?

   a. Cameroon

   b. Italy

   c. North Korea

   d. the United States

3. Which team probably surprised people the most in the 2002 World Cup?

   a. Germany

   b. Russia

   c. Japan

   d. South Korea

4. What is NOT true about the Brazilian team in the 2002 World Cup?

   a. They won seven matches.

   b. They beat Germany by two goals.

   c. They won the opening match of the tournament.

   d. They won more matches than any other team.

5. What record did Ronaldo set in the tournament?

   a. first player to score seven goals

   b. most games played in a World Cup

   c. most goals scored in a World Cup since 1970

   d. oldest player to score in a World Cup

Idioms

Find each idiom in the story.

1. **turn (one's) attention to (something)**—*stop what you are doing to focus on something else*
   - In next week's class, we'll **turn** our **attention to** Germany in the 1800s.
   - Now, please **turn** your **attention to** this painting, and I'll explain a little about it.

2. **make it (all the way) to**—*reach a final place, or one that is difficult to get to*
   - No one thought she could **make it all the way to** the top of the mountain.
   - The singer **made it to** the final round of the competition, but he didn't win.

3. **come up against**—*meet to fight or play against*
   - The army **came up against** 10,000 soldiers in that battle.
   - If those two players ever **come up against** each other, it will be a great game!

Vocabulary Reinforcement

A. Circle the letter of the word or phrase that best completes the sentence.

1. There will be eight games in the _____.

   a. tournament   **b.** matches   **c.** goal   **d.** record

2. The _____ test for the class will be two weeks from today.

   a. connected   **b.** final   **c.** ancient   **d.** unique

3. Everyone shouted happily when she _____ the winning goal.

   a. beat   **b.** expanded   **c.** leaned   **d.** scored

4. He ran so fast in the race that he broke the world _____.

   a. match   **b.** game   **c.** goal   **d.** record

5. People stopped talking about the accident, and _____ it was forgotten.

   a. as soon as   **b.** made it to   **c.** over time   **d.** turned their attention to

6. I don't think our team can _____ the team from Sweden.

   a. beat   **b.** celebrate   **c.** divorce   **d.** score

B. Complete the passage with items from the box. One item is extra.

record	scored	tournament	beaten	made it to	match

In the history of the World Cup, some teams have really surprised fans. A number of times, an unknown team has (1)_____ a well-known team in an important (2)_____. This happened during the World Cup (3)_____ in 2002. That year, the South Korean team (4)_____ the final four. Another surprise in 2002 was that a player from Brazil (5)_____ eight times in the tournament!

What Do You Think?

1. What are your favorite sports to watch, and to play? Why do you like them?
2. If you could go to any sports tournament, which would you choose, and why?

Blood Types 18

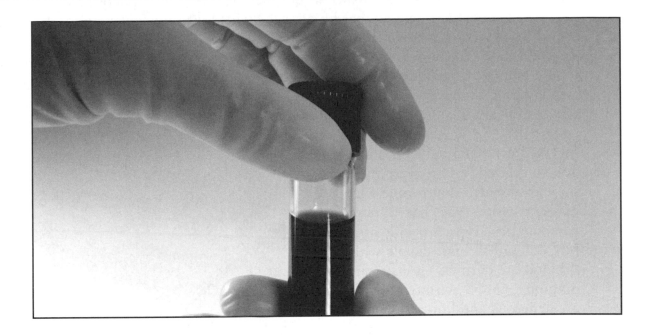

Before You Read

Answer the following questions.

1. Do you know how many types of blood there are? _____

2. Do you know your own blood type? _____

3. Do you think you can tell people's personality from their blood type? _____

Target Vocabulary

Match each word with the best meaning.

1. _____ attempt   **a.** interested in knowing about things

2. _____ curious   **b.** tells the truth and can be trusted

3. _____ outgoing   **c.** friendly and likes talking to and meeting people

4. _____ generous   **d.** different and imaginative

5. _____ honest   **e.** try

6. _____ original   **f.** happy to give

Until the early twentieth century, **attempts** to transfuse[1] blood from one person to another person were usually unsuccessful. Then, in 1901, Karl Landsteiner, an Austrian scientist, discovered that blood was divided into four types. These four blood types were named A, B, AB, and O. Blood type O is the most common
5 around the world. Blood type A is the second most common, and type AB is the least common. If people with type A blood are given type B blood, or people with type B blood are given type A blood, they will probably die.

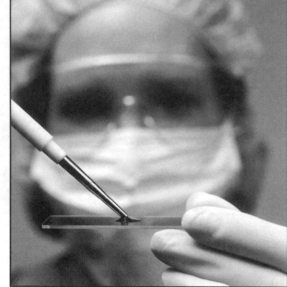

In 1927, a Japanese doctor, Furukawa
10 Takeji, carried out research and came up with the idea that people with different blood types had different personalities. Type A people are said to be calm and serious; people with type
15 B blood are **curious**, cheerful, and **outgoing**; people with type O blood are **generous** and **honest**; while those with type AB blood are caring, **original**, and careful.

20 In recent years, interest in blood types has grown in the United States, and one book, *Eat Right for Your Type*, has been a hit with people who want to lose weight.

_____ **minutes** _____ **seconds** (194 words)

Did You Know?

Almost 100% of native people in Peru have type O blood.

---

[1] **transfuse** take blood from one person and put it in another person

Reading Comprehension

Circle the letter of the best answer.

1. What did Karl Landsteiner discover?

   a. There are four types of personality.

   b. There are four types of blood.

   c. Blood type O is the most common.

   d. Blood can be transfused from one person to another.

2. What is NOT true about blood type AB?

   a. It is the least common.

   b. It was discovered by Karl Landsteiner.

   c. People with this type are said to be original.

   d. People with this type lose weight easily.

3. What is NOT true about blood type B?

   a. It was discovered in 1901.

   b. It is not the most common type.

   c. People with this type are said to be curious.

   d. It can be transfused to people with type A blood.

4. People with which blood type are said to be most trustworthy?

   a. type A

   b. type B

   c. type AB

   d. type O

5. What kind of people are interested in *Eat Right for Your Type*?

   a. people who are too heavy

   b. people with type O blood

   c. Austrian people

   d. people who are worried about their blood

Idioms

Find each idiom in the story.

1. **be a hit**—*be very successful*
   - That new movie **is a** real **hit** with young people.
   - This song **has been a hit** for a long time.

2. **lose weight**—*become less heavy or fat*
   - She **lost** a lot of **weight** over the summer.
   - I'm getting a bit fat. I really need to **lose** some **weight**.

3. **carry out (something)**—*do, perform*
   - The scientists **carried out** an interesting study.
   - The company **carried out** a survey on what people eat for breakfast.

Vocabulary Reinforcement

A. Circle the letter of the word or phrase that best completes the sentence.

1. Mike is so _____. He loves going to parties.
   a. outgoing   **b.** curious   **c.** generous   **d.** honest

2. Sarah looks great. She's really _____.
   a. carried out   **b.** come up with   **c.** on the go   **d.** lost weight

3. That artist's portraits are so _____.
   a. outgoing   **b.** honest   **c.** original   **d.** generous

4. Helen is so _____. She loves giving people gifts.
   a. generous   **b.** curious   **c.** outgoing   **d.** honest

5. You can't trust Clayton. He's just not _____.
   a. cruel   **b.** honest   **c.** original   **d.** weak

6. Young children ask so many questions. They're really _____.
   a. generous   **b.** original   **c.** curious   **d.** dangerous

B. Complete the passage with items from the box. One item is extra.

been a hit   generous   attempts   original   carried out   curious

Long ago, (1)_____ to transfuse blood usually killed people, but in 1901 Karl Landsteiner (2)_____ a study that showed there are four blood types. Many people now believe you can tell personality from blood type. For example, people with type B blood are said to be (3)_____, and those with type AB are said to be (4)_____. Books on blood types have recently (5)_____ in America.

What Do You Think?

1. Do you agree with the description of your own blood type given in the passage? What other adjectives would you use to describe yourself?

2. Do you believe in other ways of telling someone's personality, for example, star signs or palm-reading?

Television

Before You Read

Answer the following questions.

1. How many hours of TV do you watch each week? _____

2. Do you think you watch too much TV? Why or why not? _____

3. What kinds of TV shows do you most like and dislike? _____

Target Vocabulary

Match each word with the best meaning.

1. _____ broadcast   **a.** worried

2. _____ public   **b.** send radio or TV over the air

3. _____ concerned   **c.** result or influence

4. _____ murder   **d.** let or permit

5. _____ allow   **e.** of the people of a country or area

6. _____ effect   **f.** kill someone (not in war)

The first **public** television **broadcast** in the United States took place in 1928. The broadcast didn't reach many people—at that time there were only four television sets.

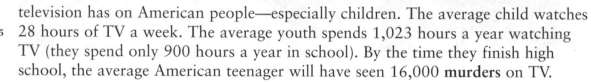

5 Today, 98 percent of American houses have at least one television, and 41 percent have three or more. The average American house has the TV on 10 for 7 hours and 40 minutes every day.

Many people are **concerned** with the **effect** that so much television has on American people—especially children. The average child watches 15 28 hours of TV a week. The average youth spends 1,023 hours a year watching TV (they spend only 900 hours a year in school). By the time they finish high school, the average American teenager will have seen 16,000 **murders** on TV.

One group trying to get people to watch less TV is the TV-Turnoff Network, who celebrate TV-Turnoff Week every year. In 2002, they got 6.5 million people to 20 stop watching TV for a week. "Turn off TV, turn on life," they say.

Watching less TV is also taking off with some Hollywood celebrities. Tom Cruise, the actor, only **allows** his children to watch 3.5 hours of TV a week. Director Stephen Spielberg only lets his five children watch an hour a day. One Australian actress, Naomi Watts, lets her children watch only the soccer World 25 Cup on TV—once every four years!

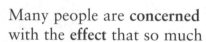

_____ **minutes** _____ **seconds** (228 words)

Did You Know?

The average child in the United States sees about 20,000 television advertisements a year.

Reading Comprehension

Circle the letter of the best answer.

1. What is the best title for this passage?

   a. A History of Television

   b. American Television Programs

   c. Can Television Be a Bad Thing?

   d. Hollywood Celebrity Families

2. What percentage of American houses have one or two television sets?

   a. 41 percent   **b.** 57 percent   **c.** 59 percent   **d.** 98 percent

3. Which of these sentences is NOT true?

   a. TV is on in the average American house for more than 40 hours a week.

   b. The average young person in the United States spends more time in school each week than watching TV.

   c. The average American child watches more than 25 hours of TV a week.

   d. The average American teenager will have seen 16,000 people being killed by the time they finish high school.

4. What is the TV-Turnoff Network?

   a. a television station

   b. a group of teenagers who watch a lot of TV

   c. the people who came up with TV-Turnoff Week

   d. a group of Hollywood celebrities and their families

5. According to the reading, who lets their children watch the most TV?

   a. the TV-Turnoff Network

   b. Tom Cruise

   c. Stephen Spielberg

   d. Naomi Watts

Idioms

Find each idiom in the story.

1. take place—*happen*
   - The contest **took place** last Saturday.
   - A race **took place** between England and Germany.

2. get (someone) to do (something)—*make someone do something because you ask or tell them to*
   - She always **gets** her children **to** finish their homework before they watch TV.
   - My boss **gets** me **to** stay late at work several nights a week.

3. by the time—*before*
   - I have to clean the house **by the time** my wife gets home.
   - Kate wants to retire **by the time** she's forty.

Vocabulary Reinforcement

A. Circle the letter of the word or phrase that best completes the sentence.

1. Excuse me, is there a _____ telephone near here?
   a. unique   **b.** concerned   **c.** curious   **d.** public

2. The police are looking for the man who _____ the woman.
   a. broadcast   **b.** murdered   **c.** took place   **d.** allowed

3. My boss doesn't _____ me to use the phone at work.
   a. attempt   **b.** allow   **c.** murder   **d.** serve

4. Alex's room was dirty, so her mom _____ clean it.
   a. allowed her to   **b.** worked out to   **c.** got her to   **d.** lost weight to

5. Harry could speak four languages _____ he was ten.
   a. by the time   **b.** over time   **c.** of all time   **d.** long ago

6. The dance will _____ on Friday night.
   a. by the time   **b.** broadcast   **c.** effect   **d.** take place

B. Complete the passage with items from the box. One item is extra.

effects   took place   public   allow   broadcast   concerned

The first television (1)_____ in the United States (2)_____ in 1928.
Today, many people are (3)_____ about the (4)_____ of watching too
much TV. Because of this, many people don't (5)_____ their children to watch a
lot of TV.

What Do You Think?

1. Do you think that TV can have a bad effect on children? In what ways?
2. Would you agree to take part in TV-Turnoff Week? Why or why not?

Rodeos

Before You Read

Answer the following questions.

1. What do you think is happening in the photo? _____

2. Where do you think it is taking place? _____

3. What do you know about rodeos? _____

Target Vocabulary

Match each word with the best meaning.

1. _____ cowboy
2. _____ saddle
3. _____ competition
4. _____ wrestle
5. _____ tie
6. _____ event

a. an important happening; a competition or contest

b. join something together with a rope or string

c. a man who works with horses and cows

d. a seat on a horse's back

e. a contest

f. fight by throwing down and holding someone

The word "rodeo" comes from the Spanish word *rodear*, meaning "surround," for a place where **cowboys** sold cows.

In the 1800s, cowboys from the southwestern United States came together a
5 few times each year in order to sell their cows. After selling the cows, the cowboys often took part in **competitions** where they showed off the skills they had learned over the past year. In 1888, the people of
10 Prescott, Arizona, began to sell tickets to these cowboy shows and prizes were given to the best cowboy acts.

Since the original rodeo in 1888, the popularity of rodeos has expanded. Now
15 people can see them all year round in parts of the United States, Canada, and Australia. The first rodeo club in Japan, the Okinawa Bull[1]-Riding Club, opened in 1998, and holds rodeos all over Japan. In South Korea,
20 the Korean/American Cowboy Association started in 1996, and holds rodeos throughout South Korea.

The most popular **events** to see at rodeos are wild horse riding with and without a **saddle**, **tying** calves,[2] and "bull **wrestling**."

In bull wrestling, the cowboy must jump onto the back of a running bull. Using
25 only his hands, the cowboy gets the bull to stop by making it fall to the ground. The cowboy who can do this the fastest is the winner.

_____ **minutes** _____ **seconds** (218 words)

Did You Know?

Every year there are over 700 rodeos held in the United States, with a total prize money of over 32 million dollars.

---

[1] **bull** a male cow
[2] **calf** a baby cow

Reading Comprehension

Circle the letter of the best answer.

1. This passage is about . . .
   - **a.** the events in a rodeo.
   - **b.** the origin and popularity of rodeo.
   - **c.** the spread of rodeo to other countries.
   - **d.** all of the above.

2. In which country was the first rodeo held?
   - **a.** Spain
   - **b.** the United States
   - **c.** Korea
   - **d.** Japan

3. How often are rodeos held today in the United States?
   - **a.** a few times a year
   - **b.** many times throughout the year
   - **c.** every few years
   - **d.** The article doesn't say.

4. Which event can a person see in a rodeo?
   - **a.** cow jumping
   - **b.** horse saddling
   - **c.** bull wrestling
   - **d.** finding prizes

5. What does a cowboy NOT have to do in bull wrestling?
   - **a.** get a bull to fall to the ground
   - **b.** jump onto the back of a male cow
   - **c.** compete quickly
   - **d.** use a rope

Idioms

Find each idiom in the story.

1. **all year round**—*for the whole year*
   - In Singapore, it's hot **all year round**.
   - **All year round**, you can catch fish in that river.

2. **show off**—*show skill or ability so other people will notice*
   - Nobody likes a person who always **shows off**.
   - The company **showed off** their new product at the mall.

3. **all over**—*in every part of a place*
   - Students in this class come from **all over** Asia.
   - There are Chinese restaurants **all over** the world.

Vocabulary Reinforcement

A. Circle the letter of the word or phrase that best completes the sentence.

1. Be careful! There's a dangerous _____ in that field.

    a. saddle   **b.** bull   **c.** cowboy   **d.** event

2. The mountain climber died because she didn't _____ her rope correctly.

    a. tie   **b.** wrestle   **c.** murder   **d.** come together

3. I traveled _____ Europe when I was young.

    a. on the go   **b.** long ago   **c.** all over   **d.** all year round

4. Jenny loves horse riding, so her parents bought her _____ for her birthday.

    a. a bull   **b.** a saddle   **c.** an event   **d.** a calf

5. Sam loves _____ his expensive car.

    a. attempting   **b.** wrestling   **c.** concerning   **d.** showing off

6. There were a few important _____ on the news last night.

    a. events   **b.** attempts   **c.** effects   **d.** hits

B. Complete the passage with items from the box. One item is extra.

events   saddle   cowboys   wrestling   came together   showed off

A long time ago, cowboys (1)_____ once a year to sell cows. After all the cows were sold, the (2)_____ had free time, so they often (3)_____ their skills at horse riding to each other. In 1888, one town started selling tickets to these shows. During these shows today, cowboys compete in various (4)_____. These include riding horses, (5)_____ bulls, and tying calves.

What Do You Think?

1. Some people think rodeos are cruel. Do you agree with using animals for entertainment?

2. Have you ever taken part in a dangerous sport, or watched one? If you were to take part in a dangerous sport, what sport would you choose, and why?

Review

A. Find words for each definition. Two words are extra.

murder   curious   allow   cowboy   public   outgoing
ancient   wrestle   attempt   original   effect   competition

1. _____ very old; from long ago
2. _____ a man who works with cows and horses
3. _____ try
4. _____ owned by everyone in a city or country
5. _____ interested in finding out new things
6. _____ a result; something that happens because of another thing
7. _____ talkative and not shy
8. _____ killing another person (outside war)
9. _____ give permission; let someone do something
10. _____ the first; different to other people

B. Complete the paragraph with items from the box. Two items are extra.

broadcast   all over   all year round   shown off   final
scores   record   tournament   takes place   matches

Soccer is the most popular team sport in the world. It is played (1)_____ the
world, and (2)_____ from somewhere in the world are (3)_____ on TV
(4)_____. Most newspapers in the world publish the (5)_____ of
important games. The World Cup (6)_____, which (7)_____ every four
years, is watched by millions of people, and the (8)_____ game of the World Cup
is watched by over a billion people.

C. Match each idiom with the best definition. One definition is extra.

1. _____ come up with
2. _____ long ago
3. _____ come up against
4. _____ be a hit
5. _____ lose weight
6. _____ by the time

a. be popular
b. before
c. invent
d. compete with
e. stop what you are doing and look at something
f. become less heavy
g. many years in the past

D. Use the clues below to complete the crossword.

Across

1. Someone who likes to give things to people is _____.
4. Jenny is happy because her team _____ the finals. (3 words)
6. a fight between two groups or countries
8. in a hurry (3 words)
10. That restaurant doesn't _____ wine.
11. a seat on a horse
12. Manchester United _____ Liverpool 3–2.

Down

2. an important happening
3. At a rodeo, cowboys can _____ their ability. (2 words)
5. join things with a rope
7. My mother has a great _____ for cheesecake.
9. not lying, able to be trusted

World Map

Countries and places mentioned in the readings:

Europe
1. Austria
2. England
3. *Brighton*
4. *London*
5. *Seaford*
6. France
7. *Paris*
8. Germany
9. Greenland
10. Italy
11. *Rome*
12. Poland
13. Portugal
14. Russia
15. Spain
16. Turkey

Africa
17. Cameroon
18. Egypt
19. *Cairo*
20. Kenya
21. Senegal
22. Uganda

Asia/Australasia
23. China
24. *Hong Kong*
25. India
26. *Agra*
27. Japan
28. *Okinawa*
29. Malaysia
30. North Korea
31. South Korea
32. Australia

North America
33. Canada
34. Mexico
35. The United States of America
36. *Hollywood*
37. *New York*
38. *Prescott*
39. *Washington D.C.*

South America
40. Argentina
41. Bolivia
42. *Uyuni salt desert*
43. Brazil

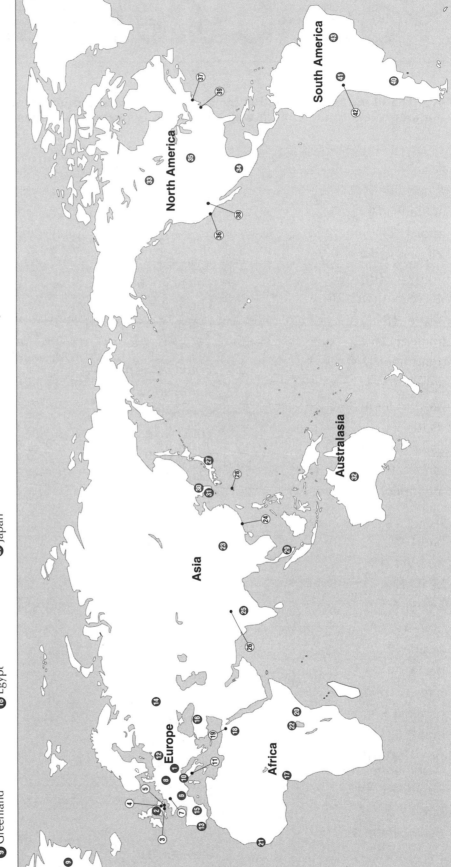

93

Vocabulary Index

Words and phrases included in the Target Vocabulary and Idioms sections are listed below. The number refers to the Unit in which the word or phrase first appears. Idioms are shown in *italics*.

A

a number of **2**
actually **16**
afford **2**
all of a sudden **6**
all over **20**
all year round **20**
allow **19**
ancient **16**
apartment **2**
apply **12**
around the world **2**
as for **7**
as soon as **4**
at first **6**
attempt **18**

B

band **9**
be a hit **18**
beat **17**
belief **6**
bell **4**
beside **7**
bet **8**
bite **1**
block **13**
brain **5**
break up with (someone) **14**
broadcast **19**
bury **7**
by accident **3**

by the time **19**

C

cage **5**
carry out **18**
cave **13**
celebrate **6**
chew **3**
collar **1**
come true **8**
come up against **17**
come up with **16**
competition **20**
concerned **19**
connect **9**
cop **11**
copy **5**
couple **14**
cowboy **20**
cruel **7**
curious **18**

D

dangerous **10**
date **14**
desert **13**
disappear **13**
discover **3**
divorce **14**
dream **8**

E

earn **2**
effect **19**
elevator **10**

end up (doing something) **10**
enter **12**
event **20**

F

fall apart **4**
fall in love **6**
fee **12**
female **1**
festival **6**
figure out **4**
fill out **12**
final **17**
find out **7**
form **12**
furniture **13**

G

generous **18**
get (someone) to (do something) **19**
get in **10**
get out of **10**
give up **3**
gloves **6**
go well **15**
go without **1**
graduate **12**

H

hide **15**
history **7**
honest **18**
huge **11**

I

improve **3**

in other words **9**

intelligent **5**

inventor **3**

K

kind of **9**

L

lean **4**

long ago **16**

lose weight **18**

lucky **8**

M

made (out) of **13**

made for each other **14**

make it (all the way) to **17**

male **1**

marble **7**

marriage **14**

match (pair) **14**

match (game) **17**

message **6**

mistake **4**

murder **19**

museum **15**

N

nest **5**

*no matter
(what, where . . .)* **12**

now and then **3**

O

of all time **15**

off and on **8**

on the go **16**

original **18**

outgoing **18**

over time **13**

P

palace **13**

period **8**

popular **1**

portrait **15**

prepare **11**

prize **5**

program **14**

prove **9**

public **19**

publish **2**

put to good use **8**

Q

quite a few **11**

R

race **8**

recipe **16**

record **17**

require **12**

role **11**

roof **7**

rubber **3**

S

saddle **20**

said to be **15**

save time/money **12**

scene **11**

score **17**

serve **16**

shout **10**

show off **20**

show the way **13**

sink **4**

stand out **5**

star in **11**

steal **15**

straight **4**

strange **9**

successful **2**

surface **9**

T

take care of **5**

take off **2**

take part in **7**

take place **19**

taste **3**

tell (things) apart **1**

terrible **10**

tie **20**

tired **10**

tournament **17**

tower **4**

traditional **16**

train **11**

translate **2**

trapped **10**

*turn (one's) attention
to (something)* **17**

turn into **9**

turn out **5**

twist **9**

U

underwear **6**

V

valuable **15**

visitor **15**

W

war **16**

win **8**

without question **1**

work out (exercise) **11**

work out (solve) **14**

wrestle **20**

Z

zoo **1**

Author's Acknowledgments

I would like to acknowledge Ki Chul Kang for his inspiration and guidance. I would also like to acknowledge Ji Eun Jung for her honest feedback from the student perspective. Finally, I have to acknowledge all of those students who inspired me to seek out materials to suit the interest of a variety of readers. It was both enjoyable and instructive for me as a teacher and a writer.

I am also grateful to the following teaching professionals who gave very useful feedback as the second edition was being developed.

Casey Malarcher

Andrew White	Induk Institute of Technology, Seoul, South Korea
Chris Campbell	Congress Institute, Osaka, Japan
Claudia Sasía	Instituto México, Puebla, México
Corina Correa	ALUMNI, São Paulo, Brasil
Evelyn Shiang	Tung Nan Institute of Technology, Taipei, Taiwan
Gail Wu	Overseas Chinese Institute of Technology, Taichung, Taiwan
Iain B.M. Lambert	Tokyo Denki University, Tokyo, Japan
Jaeman Choi	Wonkwang University, Chollabukdo, South Korea
Karen Ku	Overseas Chinese Institute of Technology, Taichung, Taiwan
Lex Kim	Lex Kim English School, Seoul, South Korea
Lucila Sotomayor	Instituto D'Amicis, Puebla, México
Marlene Tavares de Almeida	WordShop, Belo Horizonte, Brasil
Pai Sung-Yeon	Charlie's International School, Seoul, South Korea
Pauline Kao	Tung Nan Institute of Technology, Taipei, Taiwan
Richmond Stroupe	World Language Center, Soka University, Tokyo, Japan
Robert McLeod	Kang's Language School, Seoul, South Korea
Sherri Lynn Leibert	Congress Institute, Tokyo, Japan
Shwu Hui Tsai	Chung Kuo Institute of Technology, Taipei, Taiwan
Taming Hsiung	Chung Kuo Institute of Technology, Taipei, Taiwan